ZAKAT
Raising a Fallen Pillar
Abdalhaqq Bewley

THE GOLD DINAR
and the Islamic Money System
Amal Abdalhakim-Douglas

Copyright © Diwan Press Ltd., 2020 CE/1441 AH

Zakat: Raising A Fallen Pillar
incorporating
The Gold Dinar and the Islamic Money System

Published by:	Diwan Press Ltd.
	311 Allerton Road
	Bradford
	BD15 7HA
	UK
Website:	www.diwanpress.com
E-mail:	info@diwanpress.com

All rights reserved. No part of this publication may be reproduced, stored in any retrieval system or transmitted in any form or by any means, electronic, mechanical, photocopying, recording or otherwise without the prior permission of the publishers.

Author:	Abdalhaqq Bewley
	Amal Abdalhakim-Douglas

A catalogue record of this book is available from the British Library.

ISBN-13:	978-1-908892-38-6 (paperback)
	978-1-908892-82-9 (ePub and Kindle)

Contents

ZAKAT – RAISING A FALLEN PILLAR	1
The Fallen Pillar	3
Zakat and the State	4
Zakat and the Banking System	10
Other Factors in the Subversion of Zakat	18
The Fiqh of Zakat	24
The Zakat of Livestock	27
Camels	27
Cattle	27
Sheep and Goats	28
Partnerships	28
General	28
The Zakat of Agricultural Produce	29
Cereals	30
Pulses	31
Oil Crops	31
Dates and Raisins	31
The Zakat of Monetary Wealth	32
The Problem of Paper Money	32
The nisab for the zakat of monetary wealth	35
Zakat on savings	36
Zakat on trade goods	36
Debts	37

Business investments	38
Personal property	39
General	39
The Recipients of Zakat	40
The Poor	40
The Destitute	41
The Collectors	41
People whose Hearts are to be Reconciled	42
Freeing Slaves	42
Debtors	42
In the Way of Allah	43
Travellers	43
General	43
Zakat al-Fitr	45
Who pays Zakat al-Fitr	45
The Amount and Form of Payment of Zakat al-Fitr	46
The Time of Payment and Distribution of Zakat al-Fitr	46
Jizya	47
The Fiqh of Jizya	49
The Restoration of Zakat	51
The Question of Leadership	51
The Re-introduction of Gold and Silver Coinage	58
The Institution of Awqaf in Muslim Society	62
The Purpose of the Waqf	65
Types of Waqf	66
The Social Role of the Waqf	66

The Gold Dinar and the Islamic Money System   69

Introduction   71

1. Zakat: Restoring a Fallen Pillar   75

2. Trade: Establishing the Halal   82

3. The Islamic Money System   87

4. The Islamic Market   94
    Towards the Dar al-Islam   94

5. Priority Objectives   98

6. An Implementation Strategy   103
    i. Collection and Distribution of Zakat   104
    ii. Minting, Supplying and Redeeming Coins   105
    iii. Trading with Dinars and Dirhams   110
    iv. Establishing an Open Market   111
    v. Establishing Awqaf   119
    vi. Supporting Da'wa   120

ZAKAT
Raising a Fallen Pillar
Abdalhaqq Bewley

The Fallen Pillar

The men and women believers are friends of one another.

They command the right and forbid the wrong

and establish the prayer and pay zakat

and obey Allah and His Messenger.

They are the people Allah will have mercy on.

Allah is Almighty, All-Wise. Qur'an 9:72

No Muslim denies the central role of zakat in Islam as an indispensable pillar of equal importance to the prayer, denial of which is tantamount to unbelief. Indeed, Allah couples prayer and zakat together in the Qur'an twenty-nine times, and the mufassirun say that this indicates that the two actions are interdependent, meaning by that, that your prayer is not acceptable unless your payment of zakat has been properly discharged and vice versa. Yet, in spite of its pivotal nature and people's nominal affirmation of it, it is absolutely clear that the vast majority of Muslims do not give zakat the prime importance it is due.

Most Muslims realise that they should pay something called zakat. Some think that they have fulfilled their obligation in full by paying their zakat al-fitr at the end of Ramadan. Many more know that zakat has something to do with two and a half percent though few know exactly of what. A large number even attempt to pay zakat, though usually in a very haphazard way, and generally, at best, it is considered in the light of an obligatory act of private charity. People certainly do not treat zakat as if the validity of their prayers depended upon its correct disbursement and many pay no attention to it whatsoever.

This current belittlement of zakat is directly related to the impact on the Muslim umma of the historical rise of the European world order, founded on the symbiotic relationship between bank and nation state, which inflicted first colonialism and then economic imperialism on the rest of the world, and which has evolved into the new world financial order that has all but shed the political forms and geographical locations that gave birth to it.

Zakat and the State

As long as the Dar al-Islam remained a unified political reality, zakat retained the possibility of playing its integral role in the economic fabric of Muslim society. With the fall of the khalifate, however, under the treacherous onslaught of Arab and Turkish nationalists, assisted and egged on by their kafir paymasters, the dismemberment of the Muslim umma was completed and the shari'a lost its central position in Muslim society. One of the major casualties of this was the institution of zakat.

The new "Muslim" nation states were all based on kafir economic and political models and their secular governments ensured that Islam was firmly relegated to the private sphere. This inevitably denied zakat its vital fiscal status and turned it into the matter of private personal piety it has now, at best, become. But zakat is definitively a political matter not a private one. It is a matter of the public sphere not the private sphere. Its collection and distribution are a matter of Muslim governance not private charity. This cannot be overstated because not only has zakat now been removed from the public arena but nearly all the Muslims think that this is the way things should be. This is categorically not the case and failure to grasp this has been a main contributory factor to the political weakness of the Muslims in the world today.

In Surat at-Tawba, Allah says to His Messenger:

Take sadaqa from their wealth to purify and cleanse them.

The word sadaqa is used in the Qur'an both in the general sense of all charitable giving and also in certain contexts with the specific meaning of the obligatory act of zakat and the mufassirun are agreed that this ayat refers to zakat. The important point is the use of the imperative tense of the verb take. Allah ta'ala orders his Messenger to *take* zakat from the people. He could have ordered people to give it, as He does in other places order people, in a general sense, to give from what they have, but in this specific instance where zakat is intended He orders it to be taken.

Confirmation that this was how the ayat was understood is shown by the fact that, after the death of the Prophet ﷺ the Arabs who refused to pay zakat to Abu Bakr ؓ did so on the basis of this ayat, saying that, because it was in the singular tense, it only referred to the Prophet himself and was, therefore, abrogated by his death. This was, of course, nonsense since there are many ayats addressed to the Prophet ﷺ which bear a general significance. The point here, however, is that it was recognised that zakat was not to be given by those who owed it but to be taken by the leader of the Muslims.

This construction is further strengthened by the famous words of the first khalifa of the Muslims to 'Umar ibn al-Khattab when 'Umar counselled him against fighting the tribes who were refusing to pay zakat. Abu Bakr said, "By Allah, I will fight anyone who makes a distinction between the prayer and zakat. Zakat is the right which is due on wealth. By Allah, if they refuse me a hobbling rope which they used to pay to the Messenger of Allah ﷺ I will fight them for it!" The important words are "refuse me". Abu Bakr was obviously not referring to himself here as an individual but as the political leader of the Muslims and by doing so clearly shows the inextricable link between zakat and Muslim governance.

This link is also affirmed by the hadith from Ibn Abbas about Mu'adh being sent to the Yemen. Among the instructions he was given by the Prophet ﷺ are the words, "Allah has made it obligatory for zakat to be taken from their property and given to their poor." The use of the passive tense "to be taken... and given" demonstrably reveals the governmental nature of the institution of zakat, both in its collection and its distribution.

It is necessary to stress the integral connection between zakat and Muslim governance. It is not that zakat may be collected and distributed by the Muslim authorities, it is that from the very beginning it has been in the very nature of zakat that this is the case. There is certainly an aspect of zakat whereby it is an individual act of worship, in the words of a well-known definition, "the giving, as an act of piety, of a legally stated portion of one's wealth to be distributed among those categories designated by Allah in His Book," and certainly its payment is a purification of the wealth of the payers and a means of reward for them in the Next World, just as its withholding is a cause of terrible punishment, but, unlike other acts of worship, it is inextricably bound up with the government of the Muslim community.

Centrally appointed collection and distribution is assumed in the seminal books of fiqh of all the schools and this connection was taken for granted throughout the centuries of Muslim rule until the present time.

- Imam al-Sarakhsi says in his book *al-Mabsut*: "Zakat is a right of Allah and is to be collected and distributed by the leader of the Muslims or his appointees. If anyone pays his zakat to anyone else, it does not remove from him the obligation of zakat."
- Imam Malik says in the *Muwatta'*: "The distribution of zakat is up to the individual judgement of the man in charge... There is no fixed share for the collector of zakat except as the leader of the Muslims sees fit."
- Imam ash-Shafi'i says in *al-Umm* about the Qur'anic category, "those who collect it", that they are those appointed by the khalifa of the Muslims to collect and distribute zakat.
- Imam Ahmad is quoted in the book *ash-Sharih ar-Rabbani li Musnad Ahmad* as saying, "The khalifa alone has the authority and responsibility to collect and distribute zakat, whether by himself or through those he appoints, and he has the authority and responsibility to fight those who refuse to pay it."

It is thus clear that, from its origins, the collection and distribution of zakat was an integral and inseparable function of Muslim governance. All the other pillars of Islam have an interface which connects them with the central authority:

> The *shahadatayn* through its explicit acknowledgement of the acceptance of the authority of Muslim governance.
>
> The prayer through the official appointment of *khatib*s to take the jumu'a prayer.
>
> The fast of Ramadan for the official announcement of its beginning and end.
>
> The hajj for its appointed leadership.

It is, however, possible for all these rites to be carried out by Muslims who are not being governed according to the shari'a, as is made plain by the present secularisation of the Muslim world and the many Muslims subject to kafir rule in the world. (Though the lack of recognised Muslim authority makes itself painfully felt at the beginning and end of every Ramadan.) Only in the case of zakat is this not possible. Zakat cannot be divorced from active Muslim governance.

Once the vital link between zakat and governance has been severed it means that the pillar of zakat, as it has always been understood by all the Muslims throughout the whole history of Islam, has been eliminated. Any pretence at the payment and distribution of zakat in the present circumstances can only be precisely that – nothing more than a well-intentioned pretence. Denial of the integral connection between zakat and central Muslim government necessarily means that the nature of zakat has been altered beyond any recognition from its original function and practice.

Zakat and the Banking System

Another major factor in the subversion of zakat has been the change in the nature of wealth and money during the last two centuries, which also has more than an incidental connection with the change in the political situation of the Muslims we have just noted. The institution of zakat was originally prescribed for, and within, a human situation in which wealth was measured by the natural factors which had always been considered the gauge of human prosperity and indeed continued to be so throughout the world up until the end of the 18th century. Allah ta'ala delineates these things clearly in Sura Ali 'Imran:

> To mankind the love of worldly appetites is painted in glowing colours: women and children, and heaped-up mounds of gold and silver, and horses with fine markings, and livestock, and fertile farmland. All that is merely the enjoyment of the life of this world. Qur'an 3:14

In every traditional human society, the basic measures of wealth were always land, livestock and gold and silver, and it is these things on which zakat, as a tax on superfluous wealth, is levied. For this reason, all the texts dealing with zakat concentrate on these things. They talk of the different kinds of agricultural produce and the details of the zakat due on them with all the variable factors dependent on the type of produce, the quantity, the type of land and whether it is irrigated or not and many other factors. They go into immense detail about livestock and exactly what animals must be taken for zakat given the numbers and ages of the animals in each herd or flock under consideration. In respect of gold and silver, the texts specify the exact weight of each on which zakat is due and make it clear that it is the metal itself which is being taxed since it does not matter whether it takes the form of coins, bullion, nuggets or dust. The only other thing subject to zakat is trade goods under certain circumstances and the zakat on those must also be paid in either gold or silver.

The problem is that most of this has little, if any, relevance to the 20th century urban lives of 90% of the Muslims in the world today. They have no land or animals or gold or silver. That is because the vast majority of the human race no longer have any access to wealth in its natural or real forms. Any wealth we may have is in fact unnatural, or you might say unreal, wealth.

Beginning with the legalisation of usury in Europe in the 16th century and expedited by the growth of banking and the unrestricted use of usurious financial instruments and techniques ever since, the nature of both political power, personal wealth and money itself has undergone a total change in the course of the last three centuries. Real wealth, that is the ownership of the earth's natural resources, has fallen into fewer and fewer hands, while most people are left with, at best, tokens of wealth in the form of bank balances, share certificates, insurance policies and other financial instruments, with now frequently no more real existence than flickering figures passing electronically from one computer screen to another. At the same time money has turned from being gold and silver coins to being paper representing gold and silver coins to being simply paper tokens whose value is totally dependent on the whims of international speculators.

There is no doubt that usury penetrates every aspect of the financial system which now dominates every part of the globe, which means that all its instruments and institutions – paper money, credit cards, bonds, stock markets, currency exchanges – are in fact also haram. For some time the Muslims, under the protection of the shari'a, managed to stay free of the tentacles of the usurers, but first Egypt, through an unholy alliance between the British and modernist Muslims, and then the heart of the khalifate in Istanbul fell into the banker's trap, and within a short time sovereignty over the Muslims had passed into the financiers' hands where it remains to this day.

There is no doubt that the world financial system has had a devastating effect on the Muslims. It has been the means by which political autonomy has been wrested from their hands and it has removed Islam from all the day to day business and shopping transactions which form such a large part of most people's lives. It is clear that it represents the main bastion of the enemies of Islam and is where their spurious power resides and that it constitutes, therefore, the major battleground on which the fight to re-establish Allah's deen in this time is going to have to be fought. In the case of zakat, in particular, we can see how it strikes at the very foundations of Islam because it has made it virtually impossible for the vast majority of the Muslims to fulfil one of the primary, foundational obligations of their deen.

It has done this by changing the nature of monetary wealth, exchanging gold and silver coinage for paper currencies. As noted above, the zakat of wealth may only be paid with gold and silver. That it is the metals themselves which are subject to zakat and not their value as money is conclusively shown by the fact that zakat is owed on them no matter what form they take. It is further substantiated by the traditional way of treating fulus which were coins made of base metal used for lesser transactions when only fractions of gold and silver coins were required. If someone possessed a large number of fulus coins which together added up to an amount equivalent to the nisab in gold or silver, then, according to some 'ulama, zakat would have to be paid on that amount in gold or silver. But, even if they had ten times the amount by weight of the same base metal of which the coins were made, then no zakat would be due. In this case, it would mean that the fulus coin concerned was being considered as a kind of receipt exchangeable for a certain weight of gold or silver. Other 'ulama held them to be simply numbered symbolic tokens of no intrinsic value whatsoever and maintained that no zakat was due on them whatever quantity they reached.

Paper money should be considered in exactly the same light. One great traditional 'alim who saw paper money as worthless tokens was the last great Shaykh al-Azhar before the British succeeded in corrupting that great institution of learning in the late 19th century, Shaykh 'Illish. He said in a landmark fatwa on the subject:

> I was asked what is your finding as to the role of the Sultan's seal (a kind of paper money used in the Osmani khalifate) which circulates as dirhams and dinars? Must zakat be paid on it, as if it were gold or silver or merchandise, or not?

I replied as follows:

Praise be to Allah and may blessings and peace be upon Our Lord Muhammad, the Messenger of Allah.

No zakat is paid on it, as zakat is restricted to cattle, certain types of grain and fruit, gold, silver, the value of turnover stock and the price of stored goods. The items mentioned are not included in any of the above categories.

You will find an explanation for this in the fractionary copper coins minted with the seal of the Sultan which are in circulation, on which no zakat whatsoever is paid, as they are not included in any of the categories mentioned. The *Mudawwana* states that: "Whoever possesses minor coins amounting to two hundred dirhams during one year, is not obliged to pay any zakat whatsoever on them, unless they are turnover stock. Then, what he would do is to value it as if it were merchandise".

In *at-Tiraz*, after mentioning that Abu Hanifa and ash-Shafi'i demanded payment of zakat on minor coins, as both considered that what is of importance in payment of zakat is their value, and mentioning that ash-Shafi'i has two contradictory opinions thereon, he affirms that the posture of the madhhab is that it is not obligatory to pay zakat on minor coins, as there is no disagreement whatsoever that what is of importance in minor coins is not their weight, or their amount, but their value. If zakat were obligatory, whatever substance were concerned, the nisab would not be stipulated according to the value thereof, but according to the substance and amount, as in the case of silver, gold, grain, fruit. As its substance lacks relevance as far as zakat is concerned, it is treated in the same manner as copper, iron and similar substances.

And Allah, to whom praise and worship are due, is most Wise. May Allah bless and grant peace to Our Lord Muhammad and his family.

From this it is clear that, in the opinion of Shaykh 'Illish, no zakat whatsoever should be paid on paper money. It must be remembered, however, that, at the time this fatwa was pronounced, the shari'a was still in place and gold and silver coinage in plentiful circulation.

The other way of looking at paper money, equivalent to the first view of fulus outlined above, takes it back to its avowed origins as representing gold and silver. It was initially issued as so-called bankers' money in the form of a fully redeemable receipt for a certain quantity of gold or silver. In other words any banknote could be taken to the bank which issued it and exchanged for the amount of gold or silver it purported to represent. Some banknotes still retain the echo of this original function, so you find the words "I promise to pay the bearer…" or some similar statement printed on them. Seen from this perspective banknotes are in reality acknowledgements of debt – the bank owes the possessor of the note the amount printed on it. This constitutes, of course, further evidence of the haram status of paper money since under the shari'a it is only permitted to pass on debts in very specific and restricted circumstances.

From the viewpoint of Shaykh 'Illish and those like him, the only possible way of taking zakat from paper money would be to treat it as merchandise, in other words waste paper, and the amount you would need to make up the nisab makes it out of the question where zakat is concerned. If, however, paper money is understood to be a debt, then zakat definitely does come into the frame. In that case any paper money you have in your possession represents gold or silver which you in fact own but which is held for the moment by someone else. The authority which has issued the paper money owes you the amount of gold and silver it represents.

Zakat is owed on debts due to you, so, if the amount of paper money in your possession reaches the nisab and remains with you for a year or more, then you owe zakat on it, even though it in fact remains in the form of an unpaid debt. But zakat may only be paid in gold and silver; it is not permitted to pay zakat with a debt. In this situation the only way for people to pay zakat is for them to exchange some of the paper money in their possession for the specific amount of gold or silver needed to cover the zakat owed by them on the unpaid debt owed to them, which is represented by the total amount of paper currency in their possession.

From all of this, it is clear that the present world-dominating kafir economic system of banking capitalism has destroyed the pillar of zakat. This is partly because it has displaced all economic transactions into the arena of the haram by involving them inextricably in a usurious web which it is at present virtually impossible to escape. But it has done it more directly by redefining the nature of wealth and specifically by changing the nature of money in a way which prevents Muslims from paying their zakat in accordance with the conditions laid down by the shari'a.

Other Factors in the Subversion of Zakat

A further factor in the subversion of the socially beneficial and politically unifying role played by zakat in the Muslim community has been a particular method of categorising and dealing with different kinds of property developed by the Muslims themselves. In the earliest days no distinction was made between the various kinds of wealth, but at a comparatively early stage wealth became divided into two categories: apparent wealth (*amwal dhahira*) and non-apparent wealth (*amwal batina*). Apparent wealth constituted animals and agricultural produce, which were basically in the open and there for all to see, and non-apparent wealth constituted gold, silver and trade goods, which were not open to public inspection in the same way. Non-apparent wealth could become apparent if its possessor took it out of the city on the public highway to sell it or trade with it elsewhere.

At first all categories of wealth were treated in the same way with regard to the collection and distribution of any zakat which was was due on them and it was the duty of the officially appointed zakat collectors to collect all the various types of zakat from all Muslims who owed it. It was their responsibility to make sure that it reached the governmental institution of the bayt al-mal which was the aknowledged official repository into which zakat was collected and from which it was distributed to the eight categories of people entitled to receive it. Where apparent wealth was concerned this continued to be the case by the agreement of all the Muslims until the fall of the khalifate and the concomitant abandonment of the shari'a at the beginning of this century. But in the case of non-apparent wealth a dispensation was made allowing people, under certain circumstances, to distribute their own zakat on the gold, silver and trade goods they possessed.

This dispensation was certainly not an instruction, and indeed never took the form of anything more than a qualified permission, yet it is now used by many Muslims to justify the present privatisation of zakat, which in the present situation is tantamount to abandoning zakat altogether, since the other types of zakat are not being officially collected anywhere. Certainly those who take this position have played right into the hands of the secularists who now rule the Muslims in every Muslim land and have made it far easier for them to gain and retain power.

We must first remember that the dispensation was given in an environment where the rule of shari'a was total and the political reality of zakat on all types of wealth was established beyond doubt so that there was no question of the individual distribution of non-apparent wealth endangering the existence of the the whole institution of zakat as is now the case. Although it was accepted as a possibility by some scholars, all allowed, and many preferred, the zakat of non-apparent wealth to be paid to the official collectors.

The great Shafi'i scholar, al-Mawardi, said that the collector should accept the zakat of non-apparent wealth and assist people in assessing it, and some Shafi' scholars say that zakat should be paid to the leader of the Muslims in every case. The Hanafi, al-Sarakhsi, was of the opinion that no property owner has the authority to invalidate the right of collection which belongs to the leader of the Muslims, having been bestowed on him by the shari'a, and even goes so far as to say that if it is not paid to him then the obligation of zakat has not been settled. The people of Imam Malik recognised the distinction between apparent and non-apparent wealth but, as far as collection was concerned, they considered virtually all wealth to be apparent. In their view all zakat of every type is required to be paid to the leader of the Muslims via the official collectors unless he is known to be unjust in the sense of not distributing it correctly.

Another factor in the corruption of zakat has been the recent part played by Islamic charities and other similar organisations who claim to collect and distribute zakat. It is particularly detrimental because they make other Muslims think that, by giving them their money, they are discharging their zakat obligation, whereas, as we have seen, they are in reality doing no such thing. In their literature these organisations specifically ask people for their zakat and go as far as telling them how to assess it. This means that they are explicitly appointing themselves as zakat collectors. But it is absolutely clear in the shari'a that zakat collectors may only be appointed by the legitimate political leader of the Muslims; no one may appoint themselves to this duty.

According to most authorities, if a person pays zakat to someone who has no right to collect it, they have to pay it again, so not only do charities who pretend to collect people's zakat not do so, they may even have prevented other Muslims from fulfilling their obligation correctly and by doing that commit a grave wrong action in the process. Also, since they have no right in the shari'a to call themselves zakat collectors, they certainly have no right to any zakat funds on that basis, and any money collected as zakat which they then use for their own expenses has been misappropriated.

Worst of all, however, these organisations, by doing what they do, actively aid the enemies of Islam by preventing the true position of the Muslims from coming to light. By making it appear to the generality of the Muslims that it is correct and even desirable to pay zakat in the way they suggest, they collude with the enemies of Islam, whether consciously or not, by actively confirming that the present political subjugation of the Muslims under non-Muslim rule is an acceptable state of affairs.

The only way that a charity could justify its right to collect zakat would be for it to claim political leadership of the Muslim community which is impossible because to do so would entail immediately forfeiting its charitable status. Therefore Islamic charities should cease forthwith from their false claim to be collectors of zakat.

It is clear that, notwithstanding the undoubtedly sincere intentions of many millions of Muslims throughout the world, who do their best to put aside an amount of their wealth every year to fulfill their obligation to Allah of paying zakat – and Allah best knows our hearts and is able to do what He wills – the obligation of zakat, as it has always been understood by the Muslims, is not being correctly discharged anywhere. This is because the necessary connection between zakat and Muslim governance has been severed and because the zakat of non-apparent wealth, money and merchandise, is not being paid in the only acceptable form in which it is permitted to be paid – gold and silver. Zakat truly is the fallen pillar of Islam.

The Fiqh of Zakat

Linguistically zakat means growth, increase and purification. In the shari'a, the term refers to the amount of money or kind taken from specific types of wealth when they reach a specific amount at a specific time which must be spent on specific categories in specific ways. It is called zakat because the wealth of the the one who pays it is purified by it and because the payer gains increase with Allah Almighty by it, in that his rank with Allah is raised through it. This is made clear by the words of the Almighty:

> "Take sadaqa from their wealth to purify and cleanse them" (9:103) and "But anything you give as zakat, seeking the Face of Allah – whoever does that will get back twice as much." (30: 40)

The types of wealth on which zakat must be paid are monetary wealth, crops and livestock. Monetary wealth refers to gold and silver, in whatever form they take, and trade goods; crops comprise agricultural produce of the kind which can be stored for extended periods; and livestock refers to camels, cattle, and sheep and goats.

Zakat became a legal obligation in the second year of Hijra. The evidence of its obligatory nature is the Book, the Sunna and the consensus of all the Muslims. Anyone who disputes the fact that it is obligatory is an unbeliever. If someone affirms that it is obligatory and then refuses to pay it, he should be punished and it should be taken from him by force, but he is not considered an unbeliever.

There are certain conditions which make zakat obligatory and certain other conditions which make it valid. The conditions which make zakat obligatory are five in number.

- **Islam:** non-muslims do not pay zakat.
- **Freedom:** slaves do not pay zakat.
- **Nisab:** all types of wealth must reach a certain minimum amount (nisab) before zakat becomes applicable
- **Ownership:** zakat is only owed on wealth which is completely owned by the payer and completely at their disposal.
- **A year's possession:** monetary wealth and livestock must have been owned for a complete lunar year before zakat is owed. This condition does not apply to agricultural produce.

There are five conditions which make zakat valid.

- **Intention:** it must be remembered that zakat is an act of worship and requires a specific intention like all other acts of worship.
- **Collection:** zakat should be paid to a collector appointed by the leader of the Muslim community.

- **Local distribution:** zakat should be distributed among the community in which it is collected unless it is not possible to do so because none of the recipient categories exist there when it may be sent elsewhere.
- **Correct time:** zakat should be paid promptly at, but not before, the time it falls due.
- **Correct elements:** zakat should be paid with the correct means according to the type of wealth in question: the right age and kind of animal in the case of livestock; the right quality in the case of agricultural produce; and the right weight of gold and silver in the case of monetary wealth.

Although it is true that the nature of wealth has changed and that for the vast majority only monetary wealth will come into the frame as far as zakat is concerned, there are still millions of Muslims throughout the world who are involved in agriculture and animal husbandry and so, without going into too much detail, it is appropriate to give the basic rules of zakat for these kinds of wealth. The quite complex specifications involved in the zakat on these types of wealth, which are outlined in many traditional books of fiqh, show how essential it is to have officially appointed collectors who have the knowledge and experience necessary to ensure that correct and fair assessments are both made and carried out.

The Zakat of Livestock

As mentioned earlier, zakat must be paid on camels, cattle, sheep and goats provided that they reach the minimum number on which zakat is due. It makes no difference whether they are foddered or put out to grass, nor whether they are used for milk, wool, meat, riding, as work animals or for any other purpose. As with monetary wealth, no zakat is owed unless the minimum zakatable number of animals has been in the possession of the owner for a full year. No zakat is due on horses unless they are kept or bred for trading purposes, in which case they become classified as trading goods, enter the category of monetary wealth, and are assessed accordingly.

Camels

The minimum number of camels on which zakat is due is five. Between five and twenty-five, depending on the number, a certain number of sheep or goats must be paid as zakat. After twenty-five the zakat must be paid in camels of a particular age and sex depending on the number in the herd.

Cattle

All types of cattle are considered together for zakat purposes. The minimum number of cattle on which zakat is due is thirty.

Thereafter zakat must be paid in cows of particular ages according to the number in the herd.

Sheep and Goats

Sheep and goats are considered together for zakat purposes. The minimum number on which zakat is due is forty, when one animal of a particular age must be paid as zakat. Another animal is due when the herd reaches one hundred and twenty in number and then more according to the size of the herd.

Partnerships

In the case that animals are jointly owned by two or more partners zakat is owed on the whole flock or herd, provided that each partner is a free Muslim and that their share individually reaches the minimum number on which zakat is due. The zakat should be shared between the partners according to the proportion which each owns of the whole flock or herd.

General

The official collector should visit each location at a given time each year in order to assess and take the zakat from every flock and herd. The animals taken as zakat should be of average size and in good condition. If the collector is late, zakat only has to be paid on the number of animals he finds, not on the number that may have been there when zakat fell due. If the owner has died and the animals have been inherited by a new owner he only pays zakat after the animals have been in his possession for a full year. It is not permitted for the owner of animals to assess his own zakat and give it out before the arrival of the collector, but if two years or more elapse without the collector coming then the owner of the animals may assess and pay the zakat he owes to the appropriate recipients.

The Zakat of Agricultural Produce

Various types of agricultural produce are subject to zakat and they are largely those foodstuffs which can be stored for extended periods. No zakat is due on fresh fruit and vegetables intended for immediate consumption. In agricultural zakat, the nisab is the same for every type of produce namely five *wasq*s. The *wasq* was a measure which corresponded to roughly a camel-load and was a measure of volume made up of sixty *sa'*s. The *sa'* is equivalent to 2.035 litres so one *wasq* equals 122 litres. So this makes the minimum amount of any type of agricultural produce on which zakat is due 610 litres by volume. This is sometimes expressed in terms of weight as 610 kgs. The problem is that the same volumes of different kinds of produce vary considerably in weight so that it is better to hold to the volume measure whenever possible.

The amount of zakat payable on agricultural produce varies according to how the land in which the particular crop is being grown is irrigated. The basic rule is that when the land is naturally irrigated, whether by rain or surface water such as rivers or springs, then one tenth of any crop which reaches the amount of the nisab is taken as zakat. When artificial means of irrigation have to be used, at the expense of the cultivator, to bring water to the land, the zakat is only one twentieth of the crop. The zakat of agricultural produce should be assessed and collected by an officially appointed collector and none of a crop on which zakat is due may be consumed or sold until the zakat on it has been properly assessed.

Cereals

Where cereals are concerned, zakat is assessed on the amount of actual grain which has been harvested after threshing has taken place. The zakat on cereals falls due once the crops have ripened in the field and should be paid immediately the harvest process has been completed.

Certain grains are considered as forming a single category for zakat purposes, namely wheat, barley and rye. These are added together and if the combined quantity reaches the nisab, zakat is taken proportionally from each type of grain.

Other types of grain are considered as forming separate categories and are not added together for zakat purposes, namely rice, sorghum, millet and maize, so that crops of these must each individually amount to the nisab before any zakat falls due on them.

Pulses

Lentils, chick-peas, peas, and various kinds of beans are also considered as forming a single category for zakat purposes and so crops of these grown by a single grower should be added together when calculating zakat. If the combined crop reaches the amount of the nisab, zakat is due on it and should be taken proportionally from each individual type of pulse.

Oil Crops

Zakat is due on olives and various types of seed grown for their oil content. They are not added together, each being considered separate for zakat purposes. The nisab is calculated on the basis of the amount of actual fruit or seed harvested but the zakat should be paid in oil after pressing has taken place.

Dates and Raisins

Zakat must also be paid on dates and grapes when they are intended to be consumed as dried fruit. The zakat on them falls due when they are ripe on the branch but is, of course, paid after they have dried.

The Zakat of Monetary Wealth

The Problem of Paper Money

The last couple of centuries have witnessed a radical change in the way that wealth is viewed and that, rather than being seen in terms of ownership of land, and thus expressed largely in agricultural produce and livestock holdings, wealth is now seen in almost exclusively monetary terms and, concurrently, the nature of money has undergone a total transformation, gold and silver having been replaced by paper and electronic currencies. Since it is clear that the zakat of monetary wealth may only be paid in gold and silver, it now becomes a question, given the current nature of money, of how that can, and indeed if it should, be brought about.

It must be clearly recognised that, because of our inextricable relationship with the openly usurious global economic system and also because of the nature of paper money itself, all Muslims throughout the world, both have clearly moved into the realm of the haram. This is an absolutely intolerable situation and it must be the explicit intention of each and every Muslim to do everything in his power to combat this abominable system and take all the necessary steps to disconnect from it in the shortest possible time. Only then will it be possible to re-establish the pillar of zakat in a complete way.

We must, however, start from where we are, and so we must deal with the change that has taken place in the nature of money and see how zakat can be best applied to the type of currencies we are at present faced with. As we saw with the fatwa of Shaykh 'Illaysh, if paper money is viewed logically as numbered tokens worth in reality no more than the value of the paper they are printed on, then zakat does not come into the picture at all. But, as we also saw, paper money was originally intended to directly represent certain specific amounts of gold and silver, and if we take that view of it banknotes are, as was noted earlier, in reality acknowledgements of a debt owed by a bank to the bearer of the note.

From the standpoint of zakat there are two difficulties in taking this position. The first is that while this specific gold/silver equivalence was the initial intention of paper money, it is clearly no longer the case since paper currencies have long since given up any pretence of being tied to their original direct connection with gold and silver coinage. The second is that while it is true that creditors must pay zakat on debts owed to them, they do not have to do so until the debt has been repaid, since, although they own the money, they do not have full use of it until it returns to their possession. But in the case of paper money no such restriction exists because the possessors of the banknotes have full use of the value they represent by their use of them as a medium of exchange in the country in which they live, even though they do not have possession of it in real terms.

So, for zakat purposes, it is better to view paper money as being like bond certificates whose value is more or less guaranteed by the government. This does not legitimise their use as a medium of exchange, since there is no way under the laws of Islam that such financial instruments can be employed to replace gold and silver coinage as money, but it does give us a way of understanding their usage and of making it possible to assess them for zakat purposes. This is because, although they are forbidden by the shari'a, they have been imposed on us by force as being the sole means of exchange whereby we are able to conduct all the financial transactions necessary for our lives. This brings the principle of darura into play, whereby the forbidden becomes temporarily permissible if it is a question of preserving life. On this basis alone the use of paper money has gained a temporary, but extremely reluctant, permissibility for the Muslim community.

Other examples of the application of the principle of darurua are the drinking of wine to preserve one's life in the absence of water or any other permitted beverage or eating pig-meat when absolutely no other food is available. In such extreme situations these otherwise forbidden and abhorrent acts become not only permitted but in the eyes of some authorities mandatory. They are, of course, conditional on the fact that no other means exist and they must be abandoned the moment that any permitted forms of sustenance appear. Paper money should be viewed by the Muslims in exactly the same light - something abhorrent which no Muslim would use unless absolutely forced to do so, and even then with extreme reluctance, and something for which a halal replacement must be found at the earliest possible opportunity.

Although paper money may be used and therefore assessed for zakat purposes on this basis, that still does not make it permissible to pay any zakat owed in any other form than the actual gold and silver which the shari'a requires, since there is no evidence that anything else has ever been acceptable and secondly there is no difficulty in obtaining the gold and silver necessary to fulfil the obligation.

The nisab for the zakat of monetary wealth

The nisab for monetary wealth in silver is two hundred dirhams and in gold it is twenty dinars. Records of the respective weights of the silver dirham and the gold dinar have been kept from the earliest times and it is known that a dirham weighed the equivalent of 2.965 grammes and a dinar the equivalent of 4.235 grammes on the basis of a ratio of seven dinars to ten dirhams. This means that the nisab in terms of silver is 593 grammes or 20.92 ounces and in terms of gold it is 84.7 grammes or 2.99 ounces.

Zakat on savings

It is, therefore, appropriate for zakat to be taken from wealth held in paper currencies, whether in the form of actual banknotes, bank accounts, or other kinds of savings accounts, provided they amount to at least the value of the nisab and have been continuously in the possession of their owner for at least a year. If that is the case, then one fortieth or two and a half percent of their value must be paid in gold or silver as zakat. In view of the current extremely low price of silver it would seem better to take the gold nisab for zakat purposes, but whichever nisab is chosen, zakat should be paid in the metal whose nisab is selected, so that if zakat is calculated using the silver nisab it must be paid in silver and if zakat is calculated using the gold nisab it must be paid in gold.

Zakat on trade goods

Trade goods are also considered by the shari'a as monetary wealth on which zakat is due. Trade goods are all goods which have been purchased or acquired or manufactured with the primary intention of resale. There are basically two kinds of trade goods.

- Goods which are bought with future resale in mind but which may stay in the possession of the purchaser for a considerable period before he sells them. If the value of such goods amounts to the nisab or more and they remain in your possession for at least a year then zakat should be paid in gold or silver on the price received when they are sold. An example of this is the trade in Persian carpets.
- Goods subject to constant turnover, such as the stock of a shop or a market stall or any other kind of trading or manufact-uring business. When someone has such stock zakat is assessed on the basis of a regular annual valuation, on a particular selected date, of the stock and liquid capital in hand. The valuation is made on the current market price of the goods concerned. If the stock and accumulated capital combined amount to the nisab or more, then one fortieth of their value must be paid in gold or silver as zakat.

Debts

There are two kinds of debts: those you owe to other people and those other people owe to you, and both kinds of debts have a bearing on the zakat of monetary wealth. In the case of agricultural produce and livestock, however, debt is not taken into account when assessing the amount of zakat owed.

- If you owe money to others, then the amount you owe is subtracted from the amount of monetary wealth you possess before your zakat is assessed so that, for instance, if you possess monetary wealth adding up to more than the nisab but when your outstanding debts are taken into account the amount is reduced to less than the nisab, then you have no zakat to pay. If, however, you have disposable assets, which are not liable to zakat and which could be sold to pay off all or some of what you owe, then your debt is considered to have been reduced by the amount of the combined market value of those assets.

- If money amounting to the value of the nisab or more is owed to you and remains outstanding for a year or more, you owe zakat on it but do not have to pay that zakat until the loan is repaid to you.

Business investments

Investments are basically of two kinds, those whose primary purpose is to produce profit through resale and those whose primary purpose is to produce income. They are treated for zakat purposes in a similar way to trade goods. So that if, for instance, you own a property company whose principal activity is buying and selling houses then your whole property portfolio is viewed as turnover stock which should be valued annually and zakat paid on the total value. If, however, your main intention is to produce income through letting out the properties you own, then you will only pay zakat on the price you receive if and when you sell one of those properties. The basic principle applies that zakat is only due on goods or property acquired with the intention of resale in mind.

Personal property

Going by this principle, no zakat is owed on personal property such as house, furniture, household goods, transport, land which are regularly used by you and your family and not intended for trade. The same applies to gold and silver jewellery which are regularly worn and not intended for trading purposes. The same also applies to tools you own which you use to earn your living and, in the case of a business, buildings and plant used in the carrying on of the business. As mentioned earlier, however, the value of disposable personal assets which could be sold to pay debts is set against outstanding debts when zakat is being assessed.

General

The general principles of zakat of monetary wealth and they seem fairly straightforward on the surface. What you find, however, when you go into the details of people's individual circumstances, is that there are endless anomalies and exceptions and it would be impossible to cover all of them. This is a further reason why it is indispensable to have officially appointed zakat assessors and collectors with a thorough knowledge of all the laws of zakat and experience in dealing with zakat in the light of the many and varied financial circumstances which people face in the world today.

The Recipients of Zakat

There are eight categories of people to whom the collected zakat must be distributed by the leader of the Muslims and Allah, may He be exalted and glorified, lists them for us in the Qur'an when He says:

> "Collected sadaqa is for: the poor, the destitute, those who collect it, reconciling people's hearts, freeing slaves, those in debt, spending in the way of Allah, and travellers." (9:60)

The Poor

The poor are considered to be those muslims who have some means of support but not sufficient to cover their needs, so they may have a job or a business but their income is not enough to pay the basic living expenses of themselves and their families. Such people are entitled to enough zakat to bring their income up to a level which enables them to meet their basic needs. This may well be the case with a merchant whose capital and stock reach the amount of the nisab. In that case he must pay whatever zakat he owes but will also be entitled to receive zakat on the basis of his personal financial situation.

The Destitute

The destitute are Muslims who have no property and no income whatsoever. There are, of course, many reasons which might bring this situation about. It might be due to a calamity that has befallen them or a disability which prevents them from earning or they may be people who have some property to which for some reason they temporarily have no access. Students might also fall into this category if their studies genuinely prevent them from earning and they have no other means of support.

The Collectors

The collectors and the distributors of zakat are also entitled to a share of it. Such men must, however, be Muslims, free men, upright and just, and well versed in all the prescriptions of the shari'a relative to the assessment and collection of zakat. This applies even if they have other means since it is in the nature of a salary for the work they do. No zakat, however, may be given to those who are placed in the position of being its custodians.

They must be paid from other sources.

People whose Hearts are to be Reconciled

This can apply firstly to people who have just become Muslim or are on the point of doing so and who may be strengthened or swayed by help from zakat funds, and secondly to non-Muslims who are friendly towards the Muslims and who can be of some help in a war situation. This permission of the law is dependent upon close examination of the circumstances of those involved because zakat grants should only be made to non-Muslims when there is real necessity for their services or when there is a certainty of their sincere desire to become Muslims.

Freeing Slaves

Zakat may be employed to help Muslim slaves to buy their freedom. Slaves freed by this means remain under the clientage of the Muslim community.

Debtors

Zakat may be given to an individual to pay his debts, as long as these are not debts connected with the deen. This applies even to debtors who have died. Zakat to debtors is conditional on them already having handed over to their creditors all the spare money and property in their possession.

In the Way of Allah

This category is generally considered to be confined to those fighting jihad to enable them to mount and equip themselves properly. Such grants may be made to fighting men even if they are well off. No part of the zakat may, however be used for the construction and upkeep of fortifications, nor for works entailed by a defensive war, nor for the construction of warships, nor for the building of mosques or any other public works.

Travellers

Zakat may also be used for the support and repatriation of travellers, providing they are free Muslims, who have need of such help. This is dependent on them not being able to find anyone who can lend them what they require.

General

What is clear from the above categories is that zakat acts in Muslim society as the helper of last resort, a kind of final social safety net. The recipients of zakat are all people who have no access to any other source of help in their particular situation. It is important to understand that zakat is not charity. Private giving and the establishment of awqaf take care of all the ordinary charitable needs of the Muslim community. Zakat is there see to the needs of all those who have no where else to go. This is another reason why it is important that zakat should be collected communally and distributed locally since it is only communally that sufficient funds can be gathered and efficiently distributed and only on a local level that people's real needs can be properly recognised and taken care of.

A political leader is necessary in each community to oversee the collection and distribution of zakat in each locality. Normally some of the the zakat, although not a fixed share, is allocated to the collectors and then the needs of the community's poor and destitute taken care of, and then those of the other categories when and where appropriate. The decision about this rests in the hands of the political leader of the Muslims and such a leader must exist in every community to enable zakat to be distributed properly. Imam Malik puts the whole matter of distribution very clearly in the *Muwatta* when he says in the Book of Zakat in the section on those entitled to receive zakat:

> The position with us concerning the dividing up of zakat is that it is up to the individual judgement of the man in charge. Whichever categories of people are in most need and are most numerous are given preference, according to how the man in charge sees fit. It is possible that this may change after a year, or two, or more, but it is always those who are in need and are most numerous that are given preference, whatever category they may belong to.

This is what I have seen done by people of knowledge with whom I am satisfied.

Zakat al-Fitr

Zakat al-fitr is fundamentally different from the types of zakat we have been looking at previously. The zakat we have looked at so far has been a tax on superfluous wealth whereas zakat al-fitr is a poll tax, a tax on the individual, in which the amount of wealth they have plays no part. The two types of zakat are also completely independent of one another. Payment of the zakat on your wealth does not absolve you from paying zakat al-fitr and payment of zakat al-fitr does not absolve you from having to pay zakat on your wealth if you have sufficient to warrant it.

Who pays Zakat al-Fitr

Zakat al-fitr was imposed by the Prophet ﷺ as an obligatory tax to be paid by or on behalf of every Muslim at the end of Ramadan, no matter what their age, sex, economic circumstances or social status. A man must pay for all those for whose upkeep he is normally responsible – wives, children, slaves or other dependents. People who live alone must, of course, pay for themselves individually. The point is that zakat al-fitr is owed by every single Muslim at the conclusion of the month of fasting and its importance is made clear by the fact that in one hadith the Prophet ﷺ made the acceptance of the fast by Allah dependent upon its payment.

The Amount and Form of Payment of Zakat al-Fitr

The amount owed by every individual as zakat al-fitr is one sa'a of the staple food of the people in the locality where they live. As we saw above the sa'a is a measure equivalent to just over two litres, so in a place where the staple food is bread the zakat al-fitr is that quantity of wheat per person, where it is rice, then it is rice, and so on. Where various foods are eaten then it could take the form of whatever grain or pulse or dried fruit are acceptable in that area.

The Time of Payment and Distribution of Zakat al-Fitr

Zakat al-fitr falls due on the last evening of the fast of Ramadan after the 'Id has been announced and is best discharged before the 'Id prayer the following morning, although there is no harm in paying it after the prayer. It is also permitted to pay it during the last couple of days of Ramadan. It should be given to people in the community who are known to be poor. Unlike other types of zakat it can be distributed individually and does not have to be centrally collected, although there is no harm in doing that.

Jizya

The jizya is a poll tax levied on all non-Muslim adult males living under Muslim rule. Like zakat it has implications which go far beyond its primary function as a source of revenue for the Muslim government. Sanction for it, indeed the command to collect it, comes directly from the Qur'an when Allah says in Surat at-Tawba, Fight those of the people who were given the Book who do not believe in Allah and the Last Day and do not forbid what Allah and His Messenger have forbidden and do not take as their deen the deen of Truth, until they pay the poll tax with their own hands in a state of complete abasement. (9:28)

The need for the Muslims to understand the importance of jizya as a legal principle has never been been more pressing than at present. It accomplishes two vital functions at one and the same time. It makes it clear beyond any doubt that Muslim governance can only be based on the worship of Allah alone and acceptance of Allah's laws as outlined in His Book and clarified and expounded through the Sunna of His Messenger. It categorically precludes the substitution of any other premise or constitution as the statutory foundation of any Muslim society. By doing this it deals a death blow to secularism, which is overtly or covertly the basis of virtually all government in the world today.

The idea of secularism was first introduced at the end of the 17th Century precisely in order to remove Divinely revealed law from the statute books with the primary purpose of allowing the usurers free rein in their eventually successful bid to achieve world domination through the employment of previously Divinely forbidden usurious financial techniques. The justifying rationale behind the move towards the secularisation of government was that it would make the adherents of every religious faith equal under the law but what it in fact entailed, apart from divorcing government from its last connection with Divine Revelation, was making every religion equally valid and by doing that denying all religious truth.

Jizya, on the other hand, puts everything in its right place, affirming the supremacy of Islam as the final Divine Revelation for all mankind but permitting the continued existence of previous religions in the subservient position which their supersedure by Islam demands. The only way to order human society is in accordance with the extent to which people acknowledge their Creator and agree to live by the laws which He has prescribed for them which alone can ensure a justice and balance for the human race. Allah makes the position abundantly plain a few ayats after his command to take jizya when He says in conclusion to that particular passage, *"It is He who sent His Messenger with guidance and the Deen of Truth to exalt it over every other deen, even though the idolaters hate it."* (9:33)

The Fiqh of Jizya

Jizya is a poll tax imposed on all conquered people of other religions who want to live under Muslim rule without accepting Islam. The amount of the tax is four dinars which must be paid by all adult males. Women, children, slaves, lunatics, paupers, monks, hermits and the sick are exempt from jizya. It must be taken in a manner which is humiliating to the payer which means it may not be gathered collectively but must be paid by each man individually to the Muslim authorities. If someone is in straitened circumstances the amount of his jizya may be reduced at the discretion of the Muslim leader.

No person subject to jizya may ride a horse or a mule; he may only ride a saddleless donkey and then must not ride astride. He must not appear drunk in public or be seen carrying alcohol, or eat pork openly, or publicly manifest his religious beliefs or attempt to propagate them in any way. All these things incur physical punishment.

Someone subject to jizya loses his protected status and is

considered an enemy of Islam and punished accordingly if he does any one of the following:

- Takes up arms against the Muslims unless it is a clear case of justifiable self-defence.
- Refuses to pay the jizya he owes.
- Opposes the Muslim authorities.
- Seduces a Muslim woman.
- Betrays the Muslims in a time of war.
- Insults the Messenger of Allah in any way.

In return for the payment of jizya the property and lives of non-Muslims under Muslim rule are protected and they are permitted own property and carry on trade within the limits of the shari'a and they may not be enslaved.

The Restoration of Zakat

From what we have seen it is clear that in order for the fiqh of zakat to be properly applied again and the pillar of zakat restored to its pivotal position at the centre of Muslim society, two main factors must be radically addressed – the necessary link between zakat and Muslim governance and the reintroduction of gold and silver coinage as a medium of exchange among the Muslims to enable the zakat of monetary wealth to be correctly paid. A third corollary factor should be added to these two and that is the re-establishment of awqaf among the Muslims. This is partly because zakat is now viewed as charity and used for purposes that have traditionally been undertaken in Muslim society by the establishment of awqaf and partly because the re-establishment of awqaf is absolutely necessary next step beyond the restoration of zakat to the proper functioning of a Muslim society.

The Question of Leadership

In the first section we saw that there is an inextricable connection between zakat and the political leadership of the Muslim community and that when that link was broken, zakat, as originally instituted, ceased to exist. It follows, therefore, that in order for zakat to be restored it is indispensible to reactivate the the link between it and the political leadership of the Muslims.

There is one point of view which maintains that this is certainly essential but that it can only be achieved when the overall leadership of the Muslim nation has been reinstituted. In other words there can be no zakat until the khilafa has been restored because only the khalif has the right to appoint zakat collectors and oversee its distribution. It must clearly be the explicit resolve of every Muslim to see the khilafa restored as soon as possible but if we take this standpoint with regard to zakat we will be failing to take on our divinely appointed task of doing everything within our power to see Allah's deen established to the maximum extent which our situation allows.

There have been many times throughout the history of Islam when the power and authority of the khalif failed to reach many parts of the umma but that did not prevent the complete and correct establishment of zakat in those areas. When such a situation occurred the local political leader of the Muslims would stand in for the khalif and appoint collectors and organise the distribution of zakat in the region concerned. It is clear that our responsibility as Muslims in this dark time without a khalif is to do the same thing and, Allah willing, our strong resolve to re-establish the pillar of zakat on the correct foundations will prove a stepping stone on the road to the restoration of the khilafa.

Obviously the situation of the Muslims varies according to where they live in the world. In the so-called Muslim countries – those lands which used to be part of the umma when it was truly Dar al-Islam – the responsibility of the political leadership vis a vis zakat is clear. They must immediately start the process of desecularisation which zakat demands. They must start collecting zakat in the way demanded by the shari'a and this does not mean adding two and a half percent to income tax or culling one fortieth of people's bank accounts which have been the erroneous, face-saving devices employed by some ill-advised governments.

It means putting back in place the whole machinery of zakat collection and distribution and abandoning those unjust, illegal taxes by which zakat has been replaced. It means re-organising regional governmental structures and appointing zakat collectors supervised by qadis and establishing local distribution centres into which zakat is collected and from which it is disbursed to the correct recipients in each locality. And it means, moreover, reinstituting the corollary to zakat, the jizya, so that the correct relationship between Muslims and non-Muslims within the polity of Islam can be reinstated and maintained.

Since the fall of the khilafa and the break-up of Dar al-Islam a new situation has developed in the world which for the first time sees significant populations of Muslims in many parts of the world living under non-Muslim rule. Although there were isolated examples of this phenomenon before, they were rare and short-lived but, as we know, in the last fifty years millions of Muslims have emigrated to other lands, particularly to Europe and the United States, which has led to permanent settlements of Muslims in predominantly non-Muslim countries and, therefore, to a set of circumstances never before faced by Muslims in the whole history of Islam. The Muslim community in Britain is a typical example of this anomalous state of affairs.

Our responsibility as Muslims, however, remains the same wherever and whoever we are and indeed it becomes more clear-cut when we are under non-Muslim rule: we must either emigrate to a place where Islam is established and the rule of the shari'a is in place – which is not an option because there is nowhere in the world where this is possible – or we must strive to the utmost and do everything in our power to see Islam fully implemented where we are. Most communities have managed to establish the prayer and the increasing number of mosques in every city is evidence of that. Most Muslims observe the fast and many go on hajj. But as we have seen zakat is absent so it is the immediate and urgent obligation of every Muslim community to remedy that situation and put the missing pillar back in place. There can be no Islam without zakat. But nor can there be any zakat without the kind of Muslim leadership it necessitates. So our inescapable duty to implement this fundamental obligation of our deen automatically involves us in re-establishing among ourselves the political structure which makes it possible.

We have to start from where we are. Let us take the example of Britain as a case in point. It would be desirable if all the Muslims in the UK were unified under a single leadership. Then zakat collectors could be appointed from the centre and regional collection and distribution points set up and the whole machinery of zakat set smoothly in motion without let or hindrance. Unfortunately this is not the case and the various attempts which have been made to bring about this unity have been fatally flawed. In every case they have been representative organisations based on kafir models and rather than provide the real leadership which the shari'a demands they have merely acted as an interface between the Muslims and the kafir power structure and have consciously or unconsciously sustained and colluded in the subservience of Islam to kufr which is so clearly forbidden by Allah and His Messenger.

But although there is no overall unity among the Muslims, two things emerge from all the ethnic, doctrinal, and factional differences which divide us. The first is a recognition of an overriding Muslim identity, which emerges, for instance, when Islam is attacked in the media or elsewhwere, and also, crucially, clear-cut Muslim groupings on a local level which are recognised by all those who are part of them. In most places these are based on ethnic or factional divisions although there are some places where these divisions are ignored in favour of a more general Muslim identity.

The point is that these groupings do have a real and tangible bearing on the lives of almost all the Muslims in Britain, who identify with them to a greater or lesser extent, so it is at the level of these groupings that the political changes necessary for the collection and distribution of zakat must take place. Most of these groupings already have some kind of political structure, sometimes imposed from above by national organisations, sometimes based on local Mosque committees, but, however constituted, this political leadership is at present of a covert nature and entirely peripheral to the lives of most of the Muslims they pretend to represent.

Inasmuch as the Muslims actually have a political identity, it is expressed in kafir political terms both on a local and national level, dividing the Muslims along party political lines according to which party is best able to woo the local Muslim populace and expressly precluding the coming into existence of a specifically Muslim political identity among the Muslims of

Britain. The political structure demanded by zakat will immediately rectify this situation. Zakat requires overt leadership in every Muslim grouping. In order for zakat to be collected and distributed according to the shari'a there must be an openly acknowledged and accepted leader in every Muslim community. It does nor matter whether these leaders are appointed from outside or chosen from inside so long as they have the support and recognition of the community they represent.

Not only will this enable zakat to be implemented correctly for the first time in living memory it will also radically and instaneously politicise the Muslims as Muslims, endowing them with a political identity which accords with the Book and the Sunna and giving them by that token the possibility of real power that can only come about when Allah's laws are properly put into practice.

When local Muslim leadership is established in this way and zakat is collected and distributed according to the shari'a on a local basis then each individual muslim community will be able to stand on its own feet in the face of the kafir authorities and the Muslims will gain a measure of independence from their present position of total dependence on the kafir state. A further result will be that the Muslim community will gain cohesion and political strength both on a local and national level and as a consequence the Muslims will begin to see themselves in their true light as a dynamic and transformative human force rather than as a beleaguered immigrant minority.

I would like to reiterate at this point that this appointing of a leader is not an optional matter for Muslim communities living under non-Muslim rule; it is not even something which they should do; it is something which the deen of Islam obliges them to do. It is obligatory for them. No group of Muslims anywhere would think of praying without appointing an imam from among themselves to lead the prayer. Zakat and the prayer are interdependent. As the prayer is not possible without an imam to lead it, so zakat is not possible without a political leader to regulate its collection and distribution. It is therefore compulsory for every social grouping of Muslims to have such a leader to enable zakat to be implemented in the way that the deen of Allah makes obligatory on them.

The Re-introduction of Gold and Silver Coinage

In his tafsir of the ayat in Surat an-Nisa, "O you who believe! Obey Allah and obey the Messenger and those in command among you," (4:58) the great mufassir al-Qurtubi lists the seven main responsibilities of the sultan of the Muslims and the first of them is the minting of the dinar and the dirham. The pride of place given to this matter shows how important it is to the establishment of the deen and this is due in a large part to the fact that, as we have seen, gold and silver as a medium of exchange are essential to the payment of zakat. This is no less the case today than it ever has been and so it remains one of the primary responsibilities of all Muslim leaders, whether on a national or local level, to make sure that gold and silver coinage is available to those in their charge so that zakat can be paid in their communities in the way required by the shari'a.

On a national level the need to return to gold and silver is beginning to be recognised in Muslim lands at a governmental level. During his recent prime ministership of Turkey, Nejmettin Erbakan held up a gold dinar in the mosque and declared it to be the currency of the Muslims. Gold and silver coinage have been proclaimed the official medium of exchange in one of the states of Malaysia. An official announcement in the Egyptian press recently called for a return to gold currency. While this is an encouraging sign that things are moving in the right direction, it still does not meet the immediate and urgent requirement for gold and silver currency to make it possible to pay zakat as the shari'a demands. And it does not even begin to address the needs of the millions of Muslims living under overtly non-Muslim governments in other parts of the world.

The situation is not, however, without a remedy. In recent years there have been several mintings of gold dinars and silver dirhams to the exact specifications of the prophetically endorsed coinage of the early Muslims and these coins can be made available to any Muslim community anywhere in the world who are determined to see the missing pillar of Islam restored and zakat once again discharged as Allah has commanded. What is needed is for Muslim leaders to establish agencies within their communities from which these halal coins can be acquired and where they can, if necessary, be exchanged. At the same time it will be necessary to encourage all kinds of Muslim shops and businesses to accept gold and silver currency so that the recipients of zakat and others who wish to use it will be able to do so. These issues and the practical implementation of the widespread use of real dinars and dirhams are discussed in detail in the second part of this book: The Gold Dinar and the Islamic Money System.

However as with every kind of obedience to Allah and His Messenger there are likely to be benefits which extend far beyond the immediate obligation of using gold and silver for zakat. We saw at the beginning that the destruction of Dar al-Islam was largely achieved through financial instruments which removed gold and silver from the hands of the Muslims and it is precisely this same usurious world economic system that still holds the whole world, including all the Muslims, in its thrall. As long as we are enmeshed in it, it will be impossible to establish and implement Allah's deen. We have to free ourselves from it and that will only be possible by reversing what was done to us and turning the techniques of usurers back on themselves. The readoption of the use of gold and silver in the present economic environment will burst the grotesquely overinflated balloon of usurious finance and put power back into the hands of those who worship Allah and follow His Messenger.

Previously the paper currencies and other financial instruments were directly backed up by gold and silver but now that is no longer the case and the value of the currencies in use today is entirely fictitious – literally only sustained by people's belief in them. There are many examples in modern history which have shown all too clearly what happens when that belief is shaken, including the recent debacle in South East Asia. Ordinary people suddenly find overnight that the money in their pockets is worth a fraction of its value the day before. This is because it is worth nothing in itself; it has no intrinsic value. Gold is not like this. It is real. It is worth what it weighs.

Allah gives us an example in the Qur'an which is parallel to this in the story of Musa, peace be upon him, and the magicians, which is repeated for us several times. The magicians create an appearance of reality which fools the people into believing that there is really something there but when Musa throws down his staff, which is real, the sorcery of the magicians is shown up as a mere illusion and evaporates into thin air. The parallel is exact. The financiers have created the appearance of value in paper money but when it is faced with the reality of value in the form of gold coinage it will be shown up as the illusion it is – nothing but worthless pieces of paper and evanescent numbers in cyberspace. The gold dinar is truly a mighty weapon in the hands of the Muslims.

The Institution of Awqaf in Muslim Society

The restoration of zakat, particularly in non-Muslim countries, is a vital first step in loosening the stranglehold which the kafir state has over all its citizens. By re-establishing true Islamic leadership, which will for the first time give the Muslims a political identity independent of the state structure within which they live, and re-introducing gold and silver coinage, which will open the way to economic independence from the all-enveloping usurious world financial system, the Muslims will gain a breathing space which they must use to foster their strength and enable them to go on to fully implement Allah's deen once more so that balance and justice may be restored to the human situation.

But the modern state holds sway over its population by many means other than direct political control. Education, health, and social welfare form the umbilical cord which tie each individual citizen to the state, and in most cases create an almost hopeless dependence on it, making any real independence for the Muslims, which is a basic condition for the establishment of Islam, a virtual impossibility. You have the nonsensical paradox of the Islamic activist signing on to collect his dole, dependent for his provision on the very state to whose overthrow he is theoretically dedicated.

This is where awqaf come into the picture. In a properly functioning Muslim society none of these mechanisms of government control are in state hands. Throughout the history of Islam they have always been the business of privately founded awqaf, totally independent of government control. This is not a question of romanticism or looking at the past through rose-tinted glasses; objective historical research shows that education, health-care, social welfare, and indeed many other areas now considered to be the sole concern of central government, were undertaken within the Dar al-Islam by awqaf up to and even into the 20th century, with an efficacy unmatched anywhere else in the world.

What is needed now, therefore, is the de-nationalisation of all awqaf properties within the lands of the Muslims where they have been taken under state control and, in the case of the Muslims living under direct kafir rule, the gradual establishment of awqaf among the different Muslim communities so that they really will wrest the day to day control over their lives out of the hands of the kafir state structures which at present imprison them, stifling the love of Allah and His Messenger in their hearts and precluding it from being openly and graphically expressed in their lives through the implementation of Allah's deen.

In the Arabic language, the word 'waqf' literally means confinement or prohibition. In legal usage it means the non-negotiability of property ownership which is of employable value, and the direction of its benefits to a certain charitable purpose, once and for all.

There is a consensus of opinion among the legal schools regarding the validity of the waqf. Evidence for its legitimacy is taken from various sources.

- The Qur'anic ayat in which Allah says, "You will not attain to true devotion until you spend out from what you love," (al-Imran: 91), which was heard by the Companion Abu Talha, and prompted him to give away his favourite orchard as a waqf. This action was approved of by the Prophet ﷺ and is recognised as being one of the first examples of land being given as a waqf.

- Affirmative evidence in the hadith literature, such as the hadith, "A man's work ends upon his death except for three things: on-going charity, useful knowledge and the prayers of a believing child." 'On-going charity' is generally recognised as referring to waqf endowments.

- The case of Umar ibn al-Khattab giving his land at Khaybar as a waqf, on the advice of the Prophet, plus similar endowments made by other companions.

There are recorded incidences of awqaf being established by Abu Bakr as-Siddiq, Umar ibn al-Khattab, Uthman and Ali ibn Abi Talib, as well as Zubair, Muadh ibn Jabal, Zayed ibn Thabit, Saad ibn Abi Waqqas, Khalid ibn al-Walid, Jabir ibn Abdullah and Abdullah ibn Zubair, may Allah be pleased with them all.

The Purpose of the Waqf

The purpose of the the waqf is to open wide the doors of general goodwill and interest in the common good, at the same time enabling the contributors to the waqf to act out of a genuine desire to be pleasing to Allah, and to be rewarded accordingly.

Traditionally, all of the finance for the social facilities relating to worship, education, health, social welfare, caring for the poor or needy were provided by the awqaf, making them independent of the government and the safe from possible exploitation of the private sector. The awqaf also provided a secure means of livelihood for teachers, scholars, doctors and administrators, leaving them free to pursue their professions to the fullest degree. As a result, cultural, educational and scientific activity flourished.

Types of Waqf

There are traditionally two main types of waqf:

- The first type is dedicated to supporting the overall good of the people in general, the welfare of the poor, public utilities such as mosques, schools, colleges, hospitals and clinics, orphanages etc. This is made up of two parts: the institution itself and enough ancillary property or land to produce sufficient income for its permanent upkeep.
- The second type is an endowment to a specific individual, or someone's family, descendants or relatives (including one's own).

Both types are legitimate and within the recognised boundaries of the shari'a.

The Social Role of the Waqf

The awqaf have traditionally played a vital role within the social framework of a functioning Muslim society. Given that they are outside the control of both state and corporate interference, they provide a very secure and stable basis for society. Families are provided for, the poor and needy are looked after, hospitals, clinics, schools, madrasas, mosques, hostels are administered and financed by the awqaf system. The funding for these social welfare programmes is not dependent on state finance - and therefore taxes from the populace - nor on payment by the members of the public who use them. The stability of the awqaf cannot, therefore, be undermined by changes in government or changes in property values or other variables of that sort. They are outside the realm of real estate speculation.

The awqaf also contribute considerably towards cultural and intellectual growth, leaving the people involved in these activities free from the need to 'earn their living'. Teachers, students, researchers, administrators are provided for from the waqf income, and able to pursue their work to the fullest extent. The awqaf similarly perform a positive role in the establishment of social justice, encouraging the wealthy to establish the awqaf which in turn care for the needy. The voluntary relinquishment of substantial agricultural and urban properties help to reduce the excesses of wealth and poverty such as are commonplace in many major cities today.

Building on the essential first step of the restoration of zakat, which will once again base Allah's deen on its secure foundations, the re-institution of awqaf and the revival of correct business practices then made possible will be for the Muslims of this age what the ark of the Prophet Nuh, peace be upon him, was for his. When the usurious bubble bursts, as burst it will, and the ensuing flood engulfs the world, we will be enabled to float free and, when the flood-waters subside, be ready with Allah's deen to give a fresh start to the human race so that the Book of Allah and the Sunna of His Messenger will regain their rightful place at the head of all human affairs.

[1] c.f. *End of Economics* (Madinah Press), *Fatwa on Paper Money* (Madinah Press 1991) *The Return of the Gold Dinar* (Madinah Press 1996) all by 'Umar Vadillo; *Banking – Root Cause of the Injustices of Our Time*.

[2] Read the first three chapters pp 1-3 of *The Return of the Khalifate* by Shaykh Abdalqadir as-Sufi (Madinah Press 1996) for a detailed and fully documented account of the part played by the financiers' use of the usurious instruments of banking capitalism in the fall of the Islamic khalifate.

[3] See *Sign of the Sword* by Shaykh Abdalqadir al-Murabit (Murabitun Publications 1991).

THE GOLD DINAR
and the Islamic Money System

Prepared by: Amal Abdalhakim-Douglas

In the first edition I mentioned the names of several contributors. Since then the list has grown. Sometimes large, sometimes little, but important bits of information, understanding and behaviour from my family, teachers, companions and others that I met only briefly. Those far away in other lands who ran with it and put things in place to the best of their ability. People of insight and action. May Allah bless and protect them all, and reward them generously as only He can do.

This essay is produced as a reference tool for anyone who understands the real issues and has a burning desire to see the shariah in action, as it should be, and ultimately the restoration of the Khalifate.

This publication has been produced to answer the question "How?" knowing that the real answer can only be "By Allah."

Introduction

The mantra introduced in the first edition is perhaps a fitting place to start.

- Our Da'wa is Dar al-Islam
- Our Sword is the Gold Dinar
- Our Shield is the Pillar of Zakat
- Our Victory is by Allah

A lot has happened since that first edition was written and published. Institutions and initiatives have come and some gone, with varying degrees of success, impact and longevity.

A point that was certainly missed by some, was that everything outlined previously as a priority objective was something that many of us around the world were actively involved in trying to make a reality, sooner rather than later. They mistook what was written to be a book of utopian theory, whereas they should have taken it as an activist's handbook. Thankfully some did exactly that.

You will see that we did in fact mint Islamic gold dinars and silver dirhams in countries from the UK and US to Indonesia and Malaysia and continue to do so, and did collect and distribute zakat locally with these coins and continue to do so. We did have shops and other businesses accepting these coins. We did have different market projects in many places, and did work to establish awqaf. Therefore, in this new edition I have in some places added a few explanatory paragraphs. These might serve as case studies for some readers and activists as they take these matters forward.

All of what did take place was against a backdrop of the unfortunate rise of what is termed 'Islamic' banking, the establishment of the euro as a currency, the so-called war on terror, the birth and rise of crypto-currencies, international wars for resources, the revival & mainstreaming of far right xenophobia and racism, spiralling debt (individual and national), worldwide bank and currency collapses, the so-called Arab spring and the increasingly widespread verbal abuse and physical persecution of Muslims on every continent.

On the other hand the movement to re-establish gold and silver as popular and accepted currencies has taken on a life of its own in both local and international contexts. Similarly, moves to re-invigorate high streets in the UK and elsewhere seem to have incorporated a lot of what we have indicated concerning the role of the physical market. Then there has also been a wider recognition that the actual commercial contracts in play are themselves major contributors to poverty and financial injustices around the world. All of these can be taken as confirmation of our prioritisation of currencies, contracts and markets as key areas for concern.

We learned from the famous hadith of Abu Hurayrah who said, "I heard the Messenger of Allah ﷺ saying, 'That which I forbid you, avoid it, and that which I command you, do of it what you are able...'" that we are not required to implement everything all at once, only to do whatever we are able, though that doesn't stop us from trying. An inability to implement the full plan from day one is no reason for inaction. Neither can we afford to be side-tracked by the scale of the task at hand, nay-sayers, the voices of our enemies or the voices of those totally in awe of kufr and its seemingly all-encompassing system. Unfortunately those voices are likely to come from both without and within.

We have learned that the times and climate we live in are such that the twin issues of localised Muslim authority and personal wealth that zakat raises, are also two of the issues most likely to provoke adverse and hostile reactions when initially broached. This continues to be the case amongst laymen and scholars alike.

It is hoped the following will serve as a guide and inspiration for both individual and group efforts from the micro to the macro levels.

There is certainly no power or strength but by Allah!

1. Zakat: Restoring a Fallen Pillar

In the first part of this book Shaykh Abdalhaqq Bewley has given a clear overview of the institution of zakat and the basic fiqh. He also raised the matters of both leadership and the system of awqaf as being essential to the raising up and restoration of this central pillar of the deen.

> The men and women believers are friends of one another.
> They command the right and forbid the wrong
> and establish the prayer and pay zakat
> and obey Allah and His Messenger.
> They are the people Allah will have mercy on.
> Allah is Almighty, All-Wise.
> Qur'an 9:72

In recent centuries developments in the monetary and economic field have seen the introduction of financial instruments and other new phenomena, such as paper money and its derivatives which now include digital- and crypto-currencies. These have totally displaced natural currencies that are defined by their intrinsic value, which include the gold dinar and the silver dirham as well as other metallic currencies.

This global usage of paper or banking money clearly affects the way in which we approach the necessary collection and distribution of zakat. We must rely on our people of knowledge for their ability to apply well known principles of ijtihad in order to arrive at an appropriate degree of adaptation to these new circumstances. However, the degree of adjustment they are permitted to make can never extend to the modification or the abrogation of the defining principles of the deen or the operational parameters which separate it from kufr.

Although the zakat of livestock and produce is paid in kind, the zakat of hidden wealth (*amwal batina*) should only be assessed in either gold or silver, more specifically gold dinars and silver dirhams. One's wealth may be assessed by either the nisab of dinars, which is 20, or the nisab of dirhams, which is 200. A lot will depend on the custom and the type of wealth one is holding. This equates to approximately 85 grams of gold or 595 grams of silver.

However, because of the depreciation of silver prices in recent times many believe it is more fitting to use the nisab of gold as a valuation reference (unless paying zakat on actual physical gold). Indeed the prominent Tunisian scholar al-Habib ibn Tahir writes:

"Many of the 'ulama' of Tunis chose that the measure of the nisab in [paper money] should be gold and not

1. Zakat: Restoring a Fallen Pillar

silver, because the value of silver has become extremely depreciated with respect to gold. The nisab is a sign of the lowest shari'ah limit of wealth, but whoever owns the nisab in silver is not counted wealthy because of its very low value. On the contrary he has a right to receive zakah since a faqir is someone who does not possess his food for the year, and the value of the nisab of silver would not suffice for a year's provision."[1]

For zakat purposes wealth relates not only to money, but also other kinds of property including personal investments, trade goods and certain mines. Therefore, it is essential that dinars and dirhams become common enough for us to be able to use them in the first place as general units of valuation, and secondly, that both dinars and dirhams be made accessible to all Muslims in order for them to be able to pay zakat correctly.

We must be clear that the payment of zakat on wealth does not belong to the private sphere as an individual act of charitable giving; its collection and distribution are a matter of Islamic governance. Thus the key elements that are essential to the restoration of zakat as a functioning pillar of the Deen of Islam are:

a. Authority;

---

[1] al-Habib ibn Tahir, *al-Fiqh al-Maliki wa Adillatuh*, Vol. 2, p.36

b. Assessment;

c. Availability of dinars and dirhams; (and traders willing to accept them in payment for goods and services);

e. Collection;

f. Security/Storage (Bait al Mal);

g. Distribution.

It therefore becomes imperative that every group of Muslims has someone in authority among them, which implies having an amir or designated leader. If not, then someone needs to be given that authority or someone needs to take it. He must then appoint:

i. Assessors and collectors;

ii. A person responsible for the safe storage of collected zakat overnight, if necessary;

iii. Distributors;

He must also then authorise, or at least encourage and support:

iv. A supplier of dinars and dirhams to the people of the community;

v. Traders to accept them in payment.

1. Zakat: Restoring a Fallen Pillar 79

The categories who may receive zakat are stated clearly in the Qur'an. Therefore, it is important that the amir/leader and distributors are absolutely clear about these categories and who these people are locally.

In the short-term the amir may have to guarantee the redemption of dinars and dirhams from members of the community who have received them as zakat. That is if this will assist them in spending it for the immediate relief of their needs. However, the more common and accepted dinars and dirhams become, the less necessary this course of action will be.

In my own community we purchased an amount of gold dinars and silver dirhams, assigned collectors and distributors, announced the imminent collection of zakat, assigned a named assessor/collector to individuals and households, produced a zakat assessment form and held classes to help people understand the issues and calculate their own zakat. At that time we collected zakat in gold dinars and silver dirhams in the great majority of cases. Though sometimes we collected in other gold and silver media (rings, chains, bullion bars) and sometimes in cash, namely British pounds. We distributed the zakat to recipients in the same gold dinars and silver dirhams we had collected, though we made it easy for recipients to immediately redeem the coins for cash, if desired. By Allah, we did it and it continues to happens. Indeed less than 24 hours before drafting this update I was called upon to go and collect zakat from someone on behalf of the current amir. Surprisingly after working out what was due, the person elected to pay with some gold dinars that he'd been saving for many years. Alhamdulillah! We took to heart the words of the famous hadith:

> From Abu Hurairah 'Abd ar-Rahman ibn Sakhr, may Allah be pleased with him, there is that he said: I heard the Messenger of Allah, may Allah bless with him and grant him peace, saying, "That which I forbid you, avoid it, and that which I command you, do of it that which you are able, for the only thing that destroyed the ones who were before you was their great numbers of questions and their disagreements with their Prophets."
>
> Al-Bukhari and Muslim narrated it.

Many modern scholars would often talk about the whole point of zakat being to take money from the rich and give to the poor. Of course that is certainly part of the nature of zakat, but it is they who may have in fact missed the point. For the overriding motive should be to fulfil an act of 'ibada/worship that Allah has commanded us to do, and to treat it with the scrupulousness and gravity it deserves. It is the same for all the major acts of 'ibada, the pillars of Islam. Hajj may be a great social occasion, indeed that is one of its secrets, but we cannot necessarily attribute that motive to Allah's command. Neither can we say that sawm/fasting in Ramadan is commanded so that many of us might become healthier or lose weight. Yet they are certainly some of the less hidden secrets and outward benefits that many derive.

Increasingly, we found that people became slightly less inclined to immediately redeem their gold and silver for cash over the years. That was mainly due to their growing confidence that this would still be possible whenever they were ready, and also due to the wider coverage of others promoting the viability and wisdom of holding a portion of savings in physical gold and/or silver.

2. Trade: Establishing the Halal

Allah has permitted trade and forbidden usury (riba).
(Surat al-Baqara: 274)

Allah has permitted trade and forbidden usury and the people of knowledge have made it clear that the current world financial system is totally permeated by riba. Without a shadow of doubt that includes the banking system, financial institutions, stock exchanges, the very money we use and more often than not the actual forms of business contract as well as the transactions themselves.

> It is reported that the Messenger of Allah, peace be upon him, said that there are seventy categories of usury (*riba*) the least serious of which is like committing incest with your own mother.

The definition of usury is: An unjustified increment over the counter value.

It means simply that once the price or value of something is agreed or established, then it cannot be increased without good reason. A delay in paying for goods or services is not a valid reason.

Natural Trade

A purchases cocoa from B for £100 in Accra, A travels to Johannesburg and sells his cocoa to C for £150, the result is £50 profit.

Usurious Trade

A does not have any money so B says to him, "I will sell you 100kg worth of cocoa now, and you can repay me 150kg worth in two weeks." Here there is only one completed transaction, the sale, and for the delay in payment B surcharges A 50kg over and above the established value of the goods.

B has made his gains in one transaction only, he has eliminated the natural element of risk and he has done no work. His excuse for charging 50% over the value of the goods is that the payment is delayed. If B continues to sell like this he increases his stock by half every time he performs a sale. He disposes with the need to both buy and sell in the normal way. In this way the natural cycle of purchase and sale is broken; this is the effect of usury. The usurer takes in and does not give out, he consumes the lifeblood of the community without returning anything to it, his activity is parasitical. It is for this reason that every civilisation, with the exception of the present one, has always criminalised the practice of usury and shunned the usurer.

Usury occurs when:

i. Commodities are treated in a manner contrary to their nature, such as the renting of food or money (i.e. bank loans) or any other commodity which is ordinarily consumed by its use;

ii. Unnatural restrictions are placed upon the marketplace. These include monopolies imposed by law such as copyrights, patents and the concept of 'legal tender,' all of which open the door to the artificial manipulation of prices;

iii. There is no fair exchange of value for value. This means that the exchange is not based upon the free and autonomous assessment of both parties involved. The emphasis must be on 'value for value', the time factor introduced by delayed payment does not affect the value of the goods at the moment of exchange.

Legally we are obliged to accept bits of printed paper (or a digital representation) for our work and whatever we produce. This is usury, this is not a fair exchange. The banks, stock exchanges, insurance companies and the money we are forced to use are all institutions of riba. An Islamic bank is no more halal than Islamic whiskey or Islamic fornication.

Without doubt those trading practices, which have always been one of the great forces for da'wa, have been eroded and clearly now have to be recovered.

2. Trade: Establishing the Halal

Just as Europe and the world banking system introduced the euro along with all the trading and fiscal arrangements necessary to reinforce their usurious objectives, so too must the Muslims prepare themselves for the reintroduction of the gold dinar and the silver dirham along with the institutions and contracts that surround a just economy.

Muslim community leaders and scholars must take responsibility for the initial work in raising awareness of these issues and giving appropriate advice and instruction, but it is Muslim entrepreneurs who must spearhead the campaign to make the dinar and dirham a reality in our everyday lives. They have to reeducate and prepare themselves to implement methods of trading that fall **within** the shari'ah and also be foremost in supporting the proper collection and distribution of zakat. It is the Muslim trader who must begin to accept gold dinars and particularly silver dirhams in payment for goods and services, and persuade their own suppliers to do the same.

Professor Paul Collier in his book, *The Bottom Billion*, describes the nature of many international contracts as a major cause of poverty across the world. He cites mining contracts in particular, that have often been secured on the basis of bribes and unfair influence, and where workers are operating in atrocious conditions. Despite the huge sums involved it is absolutely astonishing just how often the host countries effectively end up subsiding these major corporations. Professor Collier suggests such contracts being awarded through forms of open, competitive and public auctions as a means of combatting these all too common negative outcomes.

At an individual level most of us find it difficult to challenge many contracts that we might be party to. Mortgages, bank loans, mobile telephone contracts and utility supply agreements are prime examples of this. However, rental agreements, personal loans, business partnerships and investments are all areas where intervention might be easier, and where in fact we have had some successes. Our first port of call has been the use of traditional commercial contracts that have been embedded in the deen. Qirad is the standard form of individuals investing with entrepreneurs and Shirkat the standard form of partnership agreement. Perhaps most effective has been the increased use of experienced and knowledgeable arbiters to settle business disputes between Muslims. Though more work certainly needs to be done in spreading an understanding of what a fair contact actually is (and is not). In the UK, the Open Trade Network is committed to working with partners to develop sample contracts in these and other areas and also train potential arbiters and mediators.

3. The Islamic Money System

In order to make the dinar and dirham real established currency (rather than purely symbolic), certain institutions and also certain safeguards need to be in place. It is therefore necessary to define the major institutions and concepts to which we will be constantly referring and which form some of the strategic elements necessary to enable us to achieve the task ahead.

Three key institutions of a revitalised Islamic Money System are:

i. The Islamic Mint

ii. The Wakala

iii. Office of the Muhtasib

We will also look briefly at three other important, and related, institutions:

iv. Guilds

v. The Waqf

vi. The Islamic Open Market

i. Islamic Mint

The functions of the Islamic Mint are:

- To mint the Islamic dinar and dirham in all its denominations;
- To maintain the standards of the dinar and dirham;
- To mint fulus.

Historically newcomers to a city would take their gold and silver to the mint where they would be turned into or exchanged for the equivalent amount in gold dinars or silver dirhams, for which there was a small charge.

ii. Wakala

Wakala is a chapter of fiqh detailing the conditions and behaviour of someone acting as an agent for another. On the basis of that, as an act of 'creative fiqh', some have suggested the office of the wakil, to be a Muslim of known good character operating under the authority of an amir or leader and the scrutiny of a muhtasib. In some ways it is a local extension to the activities of the mint. The functions of such an Islamic Wakala would be:

- Safeguarding and holding accounts in dinars and dirhams;
- Executing payments on behalf of account holders if instructed;

- Arranging transport of dinars and dirhams to any location in the world;
- Buying, selling and exchanging dinars and dirhams.

The wakil may neither lend nor give credit, but acts solely on behalf of others.

More recently the advent of blockchain (the technology behind crypto-currencies) has been widely touted as something that will transform the modern nature and reach of the wakala, and gold supply services in general. This may well be the case. However, some early initiatives seem to be offering a supposedly "gold backed" crypto-currency alongside a physical gold product, thus using the marketing of physical gold to sell a completely digital product. This is unfortunate, and is borderline deceitful and certainly confusing for many.

iii. Muhtasib (Auditor's Office)

The muhtasib must be a Muslim of integrity and known good character, knowledgeable in the relevant fiqh and able to spot riba (usury) in all of its many guises. He is charged with ensuring at all times the correctness of the procedures of the wakils, the markets and the mints. At some points in the history of the Muslims and in some countries, the muhtasib could to all intents and purposes have a standing equivalent to the mayor of a Western city.

iv. Guilds

The historical importance and present day possibilities of the guilds should not be underestimated. Guilds were associations of professionals formed around particular skills and industries. Thus there were guilds of, for example, boat makers, bakers and shoemakers. The heads of the guilds were very influential. They would ensure standards were maintained and competition was fair. In times of war, battalions might be drawn up from the guilds, some sufi orders would be connected to guilds and the families of deceased or injured members might often be supported through guilds. A true guild today has the potential to replace trade unions, business clubs, trade associations, pension schemes and even life insurance schemes.

v. Waqf

Throughout its history it has been characteristic of Islamic society that many of the major institutions or mechanisms were not in state hands but were the business of privately funded awqaf (plural of waqf), which were largely independent of government control. Awqaf properties include those that yield no return, such as mosques and markets, as well as those that yield income. Awqaf were not funded by ad hoc donations, neither were they institutions privately run by those who founded them. Rather, wealthy individuals would make a deed

3. The Islamic Money System

spelling out how the income generated from a waqf would be allocated to its specified charitable purposes and how it was to be maintained. In this way numerous awqaf, some large some small, provided for every manner of social welfare. Mosques and markets were themselves awqaf and would often be maintained by income from other awqaf.

The 'Third'

A major input into awqaf has always traditionally come from the third part of inheritance that someone may give to whatever purpose or to whomever they wish, many people choosing to devote it to what is called a sadaqa jariya, i.e. an ongoing charity which will continue after their death, for which the waqf is the customary legal form.

vi. Islamic Market

The Islamic market is what guarantees every Muslim the opportunity to earn an honest living. Every town or city can be judged according to the state of (or even lack of) its market. Loss of Islamic civic organisation has meant that the laws of the market, like many of the socially related issues of Islamic law, have fallen into disuse. As a result, the traditional market and its congruent elements such as caravans, Islamic commercial contracts, the guilds, and most importantly the awqaf, have disappeared from Muslim lands. These social institutions formed the core of a dynamic social ethos that was unique and enduring.

It is narrated in *Tarikh al-Madinah* from Muḥammad ibn 'Abdullah ibn Hasan that he said, "The Messenger of Allah, may Allah bless him and grant him peace, gave the Muslims their markets as a sadaqah." Meaning that they are free and that no rent can be charged on them.

It is therefore necessary to review and re-establish those laws and regulations of the market place as instructed in the Qur'an and the sunnah of the Prophet, may Allah bless him and grant him peace, so that justice and equity can once again permeate the commercial environment of the Muslims. This must be viewed as the first step towards reclaiming the sovereignty of Islam. We will look at the modern practical implementation of the market in the next section.

The goal was what we call imaret, a place for the deen. After the illuminated city of Madina, one of the most famous examples was Fatih in Istanbul at the height of the Ottoman Khalifate. If what is now referred to as Topkapi Palace was previously referred to as the "village that ran an empire," then Fatih is the place where all the institutions were on show: the soup kitchen, mosque, hospital and a host of other strategic buildings and services, the guilds, the mint and of course the

3. The Islamic Money System

market. All these elements we have mentioned as part of an Islamic Money System were on display in this beating heart at the centre of the Ottoman Khalifate, with pretty much everything being funded by specific awqaf.

Instinctively most of us know what is required. For when we arrive in a new place we do it all the time. We use whatever means we can to establish qibla, we clean a small space and put out a prayer mat. We pray one by one until a bigger space is made clean, then we begin to pray together. In the same way we must collectively begin to make a space for each of these elements.

4. The Islamic Market

Towards the Dar al-Islam

It is narrated in *Tarikh al-Madīnah* from 'Ata' ibn Yasar that he said, "When the Messenger of Allah ﷺ wanted to make a market for Madīnah he went to the market of Bani Qaynuqā' and then he came to the market of Madīnah and struck it with his foot and said, 'This is your market, so it should not be constricted nor should any tax be levied on it.'"

The existence of the market, its health and the behaviour in the marketplace have always been the true gauge of the state of the deen in every age and in every place. Historically, wherever the deen has been established along with mosques, the key infrastructures that have been put in place to give life to the new polity have included the market. This might be establishing new markets as the Prophet did in Madina, peace be upon him, or imposing Islamic rules on existing setups.

Certainly in very many places at this time, Muslims would be better served by the building of markets rather than more mosques. The impact on the life and welfare of the Muslims would extend into social and political dimensions far beyond the scope of mosque-centred activity. It is true that present circumstances might make it difficult to implement the rules and laws of the market as they should be in their totality, but this is no different with mosques. Many mosque committees already find themselves appeasing local and state authorities regarding calling or amplifying the adhan, or in many instances mosque premises are rented or leased from non-Muslims, or designated as non-religious "community centres" as a first step of establishment. We are not strangers to compromise.

In examining the Islamic Market we must not become confused or be put off by the term 'market'. Even in its limited form the Islamic Open Market can surpass the modern day shopping centre in terms of accessibility, facilities, practicality and choice. Although the exact layout can vary in different geographical locations, we suggest the following designated areas should be common to most:

- parking facilities;
- warehousing & storage;
- workshops;
- various selling areas;
- auction areas;
- office and "hot desk" facilities;
- areas for cultural and artistic displays and performances;

- public transportation access;
- courthouse;
- market office;
- toilet and ablution facilities;
- loading bays;
- mosque/prayer areas.

These elements will vary according to the size of the market, climate and local customs, which will also tend to determine how trading areas are designated. For example, you would expect separate areas set aside for fruit & vegetables and other staples, clothing, white goods, home furnishing, jewellery & luxury items, machinery, vehicle sales and auction areas. The small local seller and the big importer are both there (though not necessarily side by side) and both accessible to everyone.

The essential elements of an Islamic Market are:

- No rental charges for pitches or selling space;
- Only selling in the designated trading areas;
- No selling from workshops, offices or store rooms;
- All trading must be open to scrutiny;
- No permanent pitches, shops or stalls and no reservation of space;
- No selling of products deemed illegal;

- The supervision of the muhtasib;
- No usurious or injurious trading practices;
- The free use of gold dinars and silver dirhams or any other real currency.

The market authority will only intervene if someone is clearly contravening the rights of others or infringing the Islamic rules of trade or if there is a justifiable complaint. The political, economic and strategic importance of Muslims managing some trade channels nationally and internationally should not be underestimated.

5. Priority Objectives

With immediate effect the following objectives should be given priority status. Some are very personal. Others mean a wider call to immediate action:

1. The minting of dinars and dirhams to the specifications of the shari'ah as they were used in the first community;

2. Wherever there are Muslim communities, dinars and dirhams must be made accessible to all;

3. Muslim leaders must take on the responsibilities of office i.e. the collection and local distribution of zakat in accordance with the sunnah and, when possible, using dinars and dirhams;

4. Muslim traders and business people ought to take real steps to introduce dinars and dirhams into their commercial transactions;

5. Muslim traders ought to actively initiate and/or support local efforts to set up open markets under clear Muslim authority;

6. Muslims with personal savings or investments in banks, building societies, shares, bonds, cryptocurrencies or other

such instruments should convert them into gold dinars and silver dirhams, as and when they judge it expedient;

7. All institutions in the control of Muslims ought to begin to hold funds in dinars and dirhams;

8. Wealthy Muslims should be encouraged and aided in setting up awqaf to support all of the above, particularly when choosing worthy projects for the third of their inheritance that may be bequeathed to whomever they will;

9. All trustees or administrators of any Muslim charity or charitable organisation (including those that collect zakat) should begin to examine the possibilities of establishing awqaf to support both their charitable aims but also their running costs, including manpower. The following benefits would accrue to that:

   a. those administering the awqaf would thus legitimately be supported from managing them;

   b. the charity's expenses would also legitimately come from the income of the awqaf rather than from people's donations, which latter is not acceptable unless people donate with that intention;

   c. the Muslim community would in general benefit by the creation of ownership of the waqf property and the various opportunities that would give to employ people. Over the years we highlighted the problems caused by mainstream and 'Islamic' banks, and even verbalised our annoyance at the continuing way major Muslim charitable organisations have dealt with the issue of zakat. What we neglected to do was share our successes, no matter how small, from Majorca to Malaysia, Indonesia, South Africa, North America, and the UK. Each of these places has had success stories to talk about.

Some places did mint and distribute a lot of gold dinars. Unfortunately, sometimes that often proved the limit of their ambition. Today some of those people have morphed into cheerleaders of dubious products described as "gold-backed," rather than using actual physical gold in some form. Indonesia, on the other hand, has been a different story altogether. At the time of writing, four major amirates, several more wazirates and a host of developing communities are actively involved. Over 35,000 Islamic silver dirhams have been collected and distributed for zakat purposes. Multiples more were distributed and are being used in commercial transactions. Numerous markets and trading events have been established as well as guilds, 3,000 outlets accept the coins, and a network of over

30 wakalas.[2] They have clearly now prioritised and zeroed in on the combination of promoting local markets and using the silver dirham both as a currency and for zakat purposes.

In the UK we attempted it all, albeit on a lesser but not insignificant scale. We obtained coins, announced the zakat, assigned collectors and distributors, and duly collected and distributed zakat in gold dinars and silver dirhams. We minted special UK edition coins and we had some retailers who accepted them. We held market events where the gold dinar and silver dirham were widely accepted as payment. We also educated people near and far as part of a special UK wide Zakat Roadshow and other events. The point was that with minimal resources success could be had. Contrast this with the huge resources of the Islamic banks who primarily call Muslims to riba, or with some major Muslim charities who completely distort the nature of zakat. One can only speculate as to what might be possible with the emergence of a tech-savvy new class of entrepreneurs and Muslim activists, when they recognise the importance of these issues.

In Malaysia we could say that the number of gold dinars circulated was "off the scale" by comparison. Over £1m (a million pounds) worth of coins were minted and distributed

---

[2] see www.pasarmuamalah.net for up to date information.

over a four year period and at one point over 2,000 retail outlets signed up to accept the dinar and/or dirham in payment for goods and services. The public support of the then Prime Minister, Dr Mahathir, did not go unnoticed either, resulting in the setting up of a government owned company in the state of Kelantan working closely with eDinar and World Islamic Mint (WIM). Since then a combination of factors has seen the total shut down of most operations, with a new politically backed focus of using gold at the macro/international level in the settling of trade balances between Muslim nations.

6. An Implementation Strategy

An Activists' Manifesto

It is the command to **avoid what is forbidden entirely** and **do what we are able of what is commanded** in the hadith we saw before from Abu Hurairah that dictates our implementation strategy in these affairs. Destroying banks and burning paper money is not required. We simply do what we can to break our dependence on them. Then in putting in place what we are able, overthinking is not required. We simply push the boundaries as far as we can and the rest is up to Allah. Steadfastness (sabr) is required. The often told story that we hear from so many successful entrepreneurs is a story of repeated failure and the lessons learned, and how that contributed to later and greater success. So why should we expect to get everything right first time when involved in such a tremendous affair?

We have in the previous pages, already outlined what should be the priority overall objectives in this matter. Now we outline a clear six point strategy for going forward. Start each where you will. Circumstances will play their part, but:

- Collect and distribute zakat;
- Obtain, mint, supply and redeem coins;

- Trade using dinars and dirhams;
- Establish open markets;
- Support da'wa;
- Establish supporting awqaf.

i. Collection and Distribution of Zakat

The following points are all important for the collection of zakat:

- The Amir or person in authority has announced the imminent collection of the zakat;
- Assessors have been appointed who know how to assess the zakat correctly;
- Dinars and dirhams are available from a local supplier,
- although if they are not available the zakat must nevertheless still be collected;
- There is a Bait al Mal for safeguarding collected zakat when necessary, and from where it can be distributed;
- The Amir and appointed distributors are familiar with the categories that are allowed to receive zakat and will have been informed of those who fit these categories locally (this will be constantly updated by the assessors and others).

- Some traders are encouraged and persuaded to accept dinars and dirhams in payment, particularly in exchange for basic foodstuffs and goods such as a recipient of zakat might be in need of.

Therefore, every Muslim not himself in authority ought to place himself under a Muslim authority, and should exert pressure on that authority to implement the above process. This is the first step towards a revived Islam and must be supported by the widespread circulation and usage of dinars and dirhams (as real currency amongst all Muslims.

ii. Minting, Supplying and Redeeming Coins

Traditionally the role of the mint in terms of creating new gold dinars and silver dirhams, was that of a service provider as opposed to a commercial producer or indeed a state issuer of a currency. In other words, new arrivals in town would land with their own gold and silver coinage. They would often choose on arrival to hand over their gold to the mint or in some jurisdictions might be compelled to do so by law, and the mint would then either exchange it for an equal amount in gold dinars, or melt them down and mint fresh dinars. The trader could now readily participate in commercial transactions because his money could now be easily recognised and trusted by the general populace and local traders.

In terms of zakat, in many jurisdictions, despite gold and silver currencies in other denominations being the norm, those in authority would mint gold dinars and silver dirhams especially for the purpose of collecting and distributing zakat. This would need to be the case in the modern context. Coins would need to be produced, and those paying zakat directed to purchase the requisite amount of coins, those receiving them having the option to redeem or exchange them for whatever is common currency, e.g. pounds, dollars, etc. Redemption is needed because it is of paramount importance that zakat recipients are not prevented from deriving the benefit intended by Allah, of being able to spend on their needs without the restrictions which are bound to result until the dinar has sufficient circulation as an accepted medium of exchange.

If the responsibility of supplying dinars and dirhams for public purchase is not taken up by someone in authority then, as Yahya ibn 'Umar the well known Maliki scholar said about a similar issue, some of the community with integrity and good character have to take that responsibility upon themselves, but as a duty and not as a profit-making enterprise. Of course, they should cover whatever expenses they have, which means adding a premium on production costs when selling coins to those who require them, then conversely discounting the coins when redeeming or buying them back, which would be pretty

6. An Implementation Strategy

much in line with the way most modern gold dealers operate.

In commercial transactions gold (dinars in this case) is normally reserved for higher end transactions, silver (dirhams) for everyday smaller transactions and copper (fulus) as small change.

However, there are many added advantages of using the silver dirham as an alternative currency. Primarily, the retailer can be assured his silver coin will never be worthless, no matter what happens to the issuing authority, as in cessation of services or bankruptcy etc. The very worst case scenario is that his coin will be worth the current scrap price for silver. On the other hand, if the price of silver goes up then the issuer will likely revise the acceptance and redemption prices upwards but keeping the same differential. In this example it might mean an acceptance value of $4.50 and a redemption value of $4. Keeping the redemption differential is what keeps the system commercially viable, but also encourages retailers to keep the coins in circulation by spending them with other businesses in the network. Muslim business owners might also elect to keep the coins in order to use them to pay their zakat.

All of the above assumes a knowledge of the requisite weights and dimensions of both dinars and dirhams. There is also an established weight ratio between the coins, which is that the weight of seven Dinars is equal to the weight of ten Dirhams.

Based on the above as well as an inspection of historic coins, the standard modern specifications for the dinar and dirham are widely agreed as follows with the diameters being variable:

NAME OF COIN	MATERIAL	WEIGHT
Half Dinar	22 Carat Gold	2.15 grams
Dinar	**22 Carat Gold**	**4.25 grams**
Eight Dinar	22 Carat Gold	34 grams (almost identical specifications to a krugerrand)
Dirham	**Fine Silver**	**2.975 grams** (normally minted at 3g)
Five Dirham (Khams)	Fine Silver	14.875 grams
Ten Dirham	Fine Silver	29.75 grams
Fals/Fulus	Copper	variable

The purity of historical coins may have varied due to the source of the gold or silver and the minting processes employed. Today 22 carat is the standard used for the most popular and accepted gold coins, and fine (.999) for silver coins. However, in determining these specifications it has also been necessary to take into account the quality and robustness of the finished

6. An Implementation Strategy

product, the weight ratio of 7:10 dinars to dirhams, the weight of a mithqal (72 grains of barley) and the specifications of earlier coins that can be found in museums and individual collections around the world.

Abdalmujib Gallagher in his "Letter From India" demonstrates how important this matter of currency has always been for Muslims. He writes:

> "...Additionally, the Mughals exercised unrelenting authority over the minting of coins and refused to accept any other power's coins. Foreign traders had to submit their bullion to the Mughal mints for conversion into official coins; as soon as a boat approached port. It was stopped in knee deep water and the passengers, along with their goods, were carried directly into the customs house and the bullion would be coined next door in the mint. So the coins would be minted before the Europeans' feet even touched the ground! Most instructively, the only other Indian ruler to have had the same awareness was Tipu Sultan, who likewise was renowned for the purity, excellence and control of his coins. Tipu Sultan posed the single greatest threat to the British in India after the decline of the Mughals. His father, Hyder Ali seized the hindu kingdom of Mysore which became Tipu's power base. I visited his fort at Srirangapatnam. It is crowned by the

imposing Jamia Mosque, built on top of a large rock in the citadel. Astonishingly, on the inside, it is not much bigger than the Ihsan Mosque (in Norwich, UK). Everywhere one can see his touch, there is the mark of genius. The other, mostly Hindu, Indian chiefs allowed the Europeans a free rein to use their own coins and also to establish mints of their own..."

It should be noted that in some of these places where gold and silver rupees were in circulation they still minted gold dinars specifically for the purposes of zakat.

iii. Trading with Dinars and Dirhams

A Muslim Trade Network needs to be established amongst those who are able and willing to use gold dinars and silver dirhams, when possible, in their commercial transactions. The network must consist of:

a. Retailers who sell direct to the public;

b. Wholesalers and distributors who sell to trade customers;

c. Importers and exporters;

d. Manufacturers and producers;

e. Service providers including utilities and professional services.

6. An Implementation Strategy

The immediate issues that should form the basis of the formation of the network are:

i. Establishing fair & non-usurious business contracts;

ii. Making and accepting payments in dinars and dirhams;

iii. Paying zakat on cash and business stock.

In the UK the TIJARA Muslim Business Network was established with these aims in mind, and was a joint venture with the Open Trade Network. Since then a wider TIJARA Business Network has developed, open to all, whether Muslim or non-Muslim, in the UK or abroad. The general aims are the same but strategic business advice, support and mentoring have been added. The new look network can be joined through Olympic Sprint Business Coaching.[3]

iv. Establishing an Open Market

The Islamic Market cannot perhaps attain its highest and truest form in the land of kufr. However, it is incumbent upon us to strive to setup something as close to the ideal as possible. It will then be the main protection for whatever headway has been made in circulating the dinar and dirham on a wide scale. The market will be a great da'wa in that it will provide trade opportunities for Muslims and non-Muslims alike.

If we can achieve much of the above then we will have gone a long way towards establishing a sustainable Open Market. A simple but large warehouse with ample parking space and loading areas might be all that is initially needed in terms of location.

However, what will really bring customers to the market is choice and the 'smell' of bargains. Therefore, we should target as priorities for the market:

- Various **service providers** (e.g. shipping agents, airlines/travel agents, shoemakers, dressmakers);
- **Growers** or **major importers** of key staples (e.g. fruits, vegetables, rice, poultry)
- **Manufacturers** or **distributors** of strategic or popular products (e.g. mobile phones, computers, furniture)

In connection with the above the following points should be noted:

- Those people committed to supporting the market should ideally already be doing at least some of their trade in dinars and dirhams and be amongst those paying their zakat correctly to a local leader;
- Without itself being a waqf and without a supporting waqf the project of creating a market may need to charge at least

enough to cover costs. The real objection is to the market itself becoming a commercial project;

- In the beginning it is likely that selling space might have to be paid for, but this should be eroded as the market begins to pay for itself by renting storage space and equipment, providing other ancillary services, or the establishment of one or more awqaf;
- A buyer and seller of dinars and dirhams will have to be on site and the public encouraged to change their money on arrival. Prices in dinars and dirhams will not pose a problem to members of the public who will in the short term simply relate it to their local currency in the way one does when travelling abroad and dealing with foreign currency;
- If the necessary funds cannot be raised locally, a proposal should be submitted to the Open Trade Network who will endeavour to enlist the support of potentially interested third parties. Wealthy local Muslims should also be approached with a view to setting up a waqf or donating to support the market or parts of the market.

Over the years many one-off events have been organised to road test various concepts of the market. In some events traders participated free of charge. In others all trading was done in either gold dinars or silver dirhams, though we gave everyone the chance to exchange their coins for paper currency at the end of the day. The venues varied from indoor to outdoor, their sizes between large, small and in-between. Entertainment was a big feature of some while just a sideshow at others. Many were themed or were staged to mark special occasions. The lessons learned were invaluable, as were the direct links made with those who trade in this way for their living, Muslim or not.

To reiterate the potential and importance of the market I will finish this section with something that was originally an article written for the benefit of local politicians wanting to collaborate and understand more about the concept of the Open/Islamic Market.

Introducing The Open Market

In our opinion, there can be no doubt that both in the UK and abroad, recent years have seen an increase in financial hardship for many people. Whether rightly or wrongly the blame is often directed at the banks, government policy, corruption, multinational corporations or work-shy citizens. Whatever the root cause our research has shown that the underlying issues always seem to revolve around three key areas, namely: currency, contracts and markets.

i. Currency: From the Far East, to Southern Africa, to South America, in recent years citizens of different countries in these regions and beyond have been plunged into poverty as a direct

6. An Implementation Strategy

result of currency manipulation and speculation by outsiders. In most cases these economies have never recovered and the ordinary people continue to suffer the consequences.

ii. Contracts: Whether simple financial contracts or agreements to do with the exploitation of natural resources, the recent trend has been heavily stacked in favour of banks, multinationals and major corporations as opposed to individuals, local government or small traders & producers. In the UK, organisations and movements such as the Plain English Campaign have recognised that both the small print and also the general wording of many consumer credit agreements have left many ordinary consumers completely bewildered and thus vulnerable to some very exploitative and unjust contracts.

iii. Markets: For many producers, growers and traders, access to the market place is much more important than pricing policies or the issue of fair trade. If producers and traders are empowered to get their produce in front of the consumers or end users then they can negotiate an acceptable price and equitable terms. Cutting out unnecessary third parties ensures more money for producers who are then able to make their own decisions concerning issues of health, education and other important matters

UK supermarkets have not only dealt a death blow to many

small shopkeepers but have also impacted adversely on farmers as well as severely restricting the possibilities of success for many small or independent traders. All this in a time of increasing unemployment and cutbacks in public services and expenditure.

A major factor necessary in redressing these problems is to create vibrant, free and accessible trading spaces that give everyone in society the opportunity to make a living from trading free of charge, an opportunity that will give producers direct access to end users and consumers. We call this concept the Open Market

We think that our concept of the **Open Market** can radically change and regenerate communities and society in general for the better, and in so doing directly tackle issues of poverty, isolation and unemployment. The Open Market can cater for 2,000 independent traders in less space than a shopping centre currently catering for just 100 shops. The Open Market will be able to offer greater choice and lower prices, naturally support local producers, support existing businesses and be a hive of social activity and interaction.

Many reports and a great deal of research point to the beneficial effect of markets in general on the population.

(1) **Markets as social spaces**

6. An Implementation Strategy

Joseph Rowntree Foundation

The team found that:

- Markets were important sites of social interaction for all groups in the community, but most significantly for older people, especially women. Markets also represented important social spaces for mothers with young children, young people, and families with children, particularly at weekends.

- Markets had a significant social inclusion role, as places to linger, particularly for older people and young mothers. Some markets also appeared to be inclusive of disabled people, although in other places this was less evident.

- The social life of traders played a significant role in creating a vibrant atmosphere in markets, and in forging social bonds and links in the trading community as well as with shopping centre regeneration and healthy eating.[4]

(2) The Portas Review - An independent review into the future of our high streets

UK Department for Business, Innovation and Skills

Points four and five in the executive summary recommend the following actions:

---

4   https://www.jrf.org.uk/report/markets-social-spaces

- Establish a new "National Market Day" where budding shopkeepers can try their hand at operating a low-cost retail business.

- Make it easier for people to become market traders by removing unnecessary regulations so that anyone can trade on the high street unless there is a valid reason why not.[5]

(3) **The World on a Plate: Queens Market - The Economic and social value of London's most ethnically diverse street market**

New Economics Foundation

The report finds that:

- **A 'shopping basket' exercise found that items bought at the market were on average 53 per cent cheaper than at a local ASDA/Wal-Mart supermarket.** Moreover, the market offers particular benefits to low-income customers not available at supermarkets. They can use the bargaining and haggling culture to achieve substantial discounts. This process reaches a climax at the end of the market day where produce is reduced to clear or given away free rather than left to waste.[6]

---

5   https://www.gov.uk/government/publications/the-portas-review-the-future-of-our-high-streets

6   https://neweconomics.org/2006/05/the-world-on-a-plate

These are just a few of many examples of research that supports our vision of an Open Market and which we have found to be useful in gaining support from local government in particular and other institutions.

v. Establishing Awqaf

The concept underlying the major charitable foundations that are prevalent in the UK and elsewhere is said to be firmly based on the model of the waqf, the Islamic charitable entity that has been a fundamental part of Muslim society from the earliest times.

It makes sense for Muslim leaders to encourage and facilitate wealthy Muslims and entrepreneurs in setting up awqaf. In the first instance it is simply to remind people that an on-going sadaqa in this world is one of those things that will benefit each of us in the next world. Establishing awqaf is one of the best ways to achieve that. Also, if not the main recipients, family members can also be written in to the management document and thus become beneficiaries through management fees etc. In most places modern charitable laws and models can be used as a viable framework, perhaps by those who already draft Islamic wills.

vi. Supporting Da'wa

Everything we have mentioned so far supports any serious movement towards the establishment of a place for the deen of Islam, whether this be in Europe, the Americas, Africa, Asia or elsewhere. Though in recent years (even decades) significant events have changed the political landscape irrevocably, the result has been two-fold: first, this has allowed governments around the world to attack their Muslim populations with seeming impunity, blaming "radicalisation" along with an infiltration of extremists or terrorists; second, Muslim populations themselves withdrawing from the open use of terms like Dar al-Islam for fear of excessive monitoring, scrutiny, or being labelled terrorist sympathisers or supporters. Consequently both the message of this book and the justice of Islam have largely been forgotten or deliberately ignored. Muslims themselves have overlooked the fact that the deen consists of both 'ibadat and mu'amalat, 'ibadat being the transactions between ourselves and Allah, such as the prayer, zakat, fasting and hajj, and mu'amalat being transactions between each other, such as marriage, divorce and business transactions. It is clear that over the years many non-Muslim voices have heard our critique, picked it up, run with it and become known as progressive visionaries. They talk about new towns. They talk about revitalising the high streets by offering free spaces to traders. They talk about gold and silver as currency. They talk about new local currencies.

Our duties most certainly include spreading the message of tawhid, the oneness of Allah, and to do this as we remember:

- Our Da'wa is Dar al-Islam.
- Our Sword is the Gold Dinar
- Our Shield is the Pillar of Zakat
- Our Victory is by Allah.

May Allah give us all success!

www.ingramcontent.com/pod-product-compliance
Lightning Source LLC
Chambersburg PA
CBHW071708040426
42446CB00011B/1963